Housing

with Number & Types of Units.

1. **Crossroads** (Everett)
   6 Affordable rent, 5 shelter
2. **Kennedy Court** (Everett)
   7 Homeless, 1 affordable rent
3. **Harrison Apts** (Everett)
   8 Homeless, 1 affordable rent
4. **Arlington Triplex** (Arlington)
   1 Affordable rent, 2 homeless
5. **Gold Bar** (Gold Bar)
   8 Homeownership
6. **Lake Alyson** (Granite Falls)
   16 Homeownership
7. **Blue Spruce** (Granite Falls)
   16 Homeownership
8. **Lake Howard** (Seven Lakes)
   16 Homeownership
9. **Timber Park** (Arlington)
   25 Homeownership
10. **Avanti House** (Lake Stevens)
    1 Affordable rent, 2 homeless
11. **Commerce Building** (Everett)
    48 Affordable rent
12. **Lervick Family Village** (Stanwood)
    7 Affordable rent, 6 homeless,
    1 shelter
13. **Hope Village I** (Everett)
    6 Affordable rent, 13 homeless
14. **Vision House** (Lake Stevens)
    1 Affordable rent
15. **Beachwood** (Marysville)
    20 Affordable rent, 5 homeless
16. **Oakes Commons** (Everett)
    20 Affordable rent
17. **Country Manor** (Arlington)
    29 Homeownership
18. **Highland View Estates** (Arlington)
    8 Homeownership
19. **Bogart Meadows** (Granite Falls)
    10 Homeownership
20. **New Century Village** (Everett)
    18 Affordable rent, 26 homeless
21. **The Bluff** (Arlington)
    32 Homeownership
22. **Maple Leaf Meadows** (Arlington)
    9 Affordable rent, 12 homeless
23. **Avondale** (Everett)
    14 Homeless
24. **Winter's Creek South** (Sultan)
    2 Affordable rent, 3 homeless
25. **Hope Village II** (Everett)
    3 Affordable rent, 9 homeless
26. **Winter's Creek North** (Sultan)
    11 homeless
27. **Fleming Duplexes** (Everett)
    6 Affordable rent
28. **Port Susan** (Stanwood)
    20 Homeownership
29. **Woods Creek** (Monroe)
    2 Affordable rent, 6 homeless
30. **Sky Meadows West** (Monroe)
    8 Homeownership
31. **Sky Meadows East** (Monroe)
    8 Homeownership
32. **Mission Highlands** (Tulalip)
    5 Homeownership
33. **Mt. Baker View** (Everett)
    20 Affordable rent
34. **Copper Station** (Stanwood)
    35 Homeownership
35. **Lincoln Hill Village** (Stanwood)
    19 Affordable rent, 5 homeless
36. **Park Place Townhomes** (Marysville)
    14 Affordable rent
37. **Marvin Gardens** (Monroe)
    5 Homeownership
38. **Pilchuck Place** (Snohomish)
    10 Affordable rent

Housing Type Legend

- Shelter, Homeless and Affordable Rent Units
- Affordable Rent Units
- Home Ownership (Team HomeBuilding)

Housing Hope's Service-Enriched Housing Continuum:

Shelter – Emergency Shelter for up to a 90 day occupancy.

Homeless – Apartments with comprehensive services for homeless families with children.

Affordable rent – Apartments affordable for families with low incomes.

Homeownership – Team HomeBuilding sweat-equity homeownership for low income households.

Housing Hope Village, original painting by Bernie Webber

Building HOPE

the first 25 years of Housing Hope

Written by David M. Buerge

Foreword by Edwin R. Petersen
Founding Executive Director

Epilogue by William H. Gates, Sr.

***Dedicated** – To our volunteers, donors and staff who have offered a 'hand up'; and to our families who have taken that hand to resolve their homelessness.*

Thank you ***to the following Book Sponsors:***

BECU
Boeing
Dykeman
The Everett Clinic
Union Bank

Table *of Contents* *Pages*

Foreword	Edwin R. Petersen	**6**
Chapter 1	Beginnings: 1987-1988	**9**
Chapter 2	Vision In Action: 1988-1989	**27**
Chapter 3	Running Uphill: 1990-1994	**41**
Chapter 4	Building Hope And A Village: 1994-2000	**57**
Chapter 5	Into The New Millennium: 2000-2007	**81**
Chapter 6	Into The Great Recession: 2007-2012	**97**
Epilogue	William H. Gates, Sr.	**118**
Appendix	The Housing Hope Model	**121**
Credits		**134**
Award Recipients		**136**
Index		**138**
Twenty-Five Significant Events 1987-2012		**142**

Kids Artwork *– At the end of each chapter is a drawing by a homeless child from Tomorrow's Hope Child Development Center depicting the home hoped for in the future.*

Foreword *by Edwin R. Petersen*

It hit our community unexpectedly. Not since the great depression had we seen such a thing. Homeless families with children were sleeping in cars, tents and motels. Jails had become the new mental hospitals because "three meals and a cot" was preferable to sleeping on the streets for de-institutionalized mentally ill individuals. It was the early 1980s.

The stars were badly aligned for affordable housing. Gentrification was taking out large numbers of the most affordable housing units for conversion to "higher and better uses". The federal government was dramatically reducing its investment in affordable housing under the new "federalism" which sought to transfer significant government functions to the local level. The decrease in supply and increasing demand caused rents to increase rapidly and significantly. Wages were stagnant. Family homelessness was the result.

Two compelling themes emerged as an action plan was formulated. First, a safe, secure home was determined to be the real solution, not another emergency shelter. Second, a program was needed to *rebuild hope* and replace the despair of struggling families with a renewed sense of possibilities. The organization was named Housing Hope to represent these two themes. In implementing these values Housing Hope became the story of a *community in action*. It's a story of local people who took the issue of homelessness into their own hands to create a local solution.

The question on our minds was this. *How does a community mobilize to address a social issue of the magnitude of homeless families and affordable housing?* The challenge was to capture, organize and energize the latent urge to action generated by the reality of homeless families and the vividness of their poignant stories.

Crisis creates opportunity. This was our mantra from inception. Citizens were frustrated. Families were arriving at the front door of downtown churches desperate for help. Motel vouchers paid by churches were quickly depleting mission funds without providing any real solution. The only shelter in town was splitting up families with female and male members into separate mission facilities at precisely the time when families need to be together. Sleeping in cars and camping out was fraught with public safety and health concerns.

The North Snohomish County Association of Churches, made up of Methodists, Presbyterians, Lutherans, Congregationalists and Catholics, formed during the week of Epiphany in 1984, rose to the challenge. Four years of social issue workshops and special projects finally culminated in the founding of Snohomish County's first ever nonprofit Housing Development Corporation, Housing Hope.

From its inception, Housing Hope was grassroots, engaging citizens everywhere to be a part of the solution. The **mission** was to serve the lowest income segment of the community. The **solution** was safe, secure, affordable housing, not temporary band aid assistance. The **approach** was one family at a time. The program had a dream. We wanted a comprehensive program of resources to help residents secure housing and overcome obstacles to their stability. The **vision** was pathways toward self-sufficiency for vulnerable neighbors. The **operational philosophy** was to be inclusive by welcoming anyone who cared about the issue to contribute time, talent or treasure.

Housing Hope had much to learn. We listened to the "people" (residents, homeless families, faith communities, community leaders) and they taught us what was needed. Housing Hope then did two things. First, it articulated the community's vision. Second, it served as a steward of the people's resources to implement programs that the community desired.

The Housing Hope history flows through the villages and towns of Snohomish County and its institutions of faith, business and government. The evolution was organic and opportunistic but carefully crafted to fill in components of Housing Hope's well thought out service-enriched housing continuum. Twenty-five years later this little startup entity, thought up in the basements of local churches, has captured the imagination of the local community as well as communities far and wide. It is well on its way to achieving its organizational aspiration:

"Housing Hope will be the best locally-based service enriched housing continuum in the world."

This book has a dual purpose. It celebrates 25 years of amazing results. It seeks to inspire other communities to set lofty goals to address social ills.

Edwin R. Petersen
Founding Executive Director

"...Every movement needs a catalyst. For us it was people of faith. Local congregations found homeless families at their front door and wanted better for their neighbors. The biblical message in the Letter of James was a guiding reference."

Edwin R. Petersen
Founding Executive Director

James 1:23

For if any are hearers of the word and not doers, they are like those who look at themselves in a mirror; for they look at themselves and, on going away, immediately forget what they were like. But those who look into the perfect law, the law of liberty, and persevere, being not hearers who forget but doers who act—they will be blessed in their doing... Religion that is pure...is this: to visit orphans and widows in their affliction.

(above) The founding board members in 1997. Pictured left to right: Todd Morrow, Mae Stork, Amy Youngstrom, Bruce Eklund and Jon Witte.
(right) The founding board members in 2012. Mae passed away in 2004 and Amy in 2012.

Artist depiction of the original house on Pigeon Creek by 12 year old Zachary and his mother Elaine Petersen

Chapter 1 Beginnings: 1987-1988

> *"...Never doubt that a small group of thoughtful, committed citizens can change the world. Indeed, it is the only thing that ever has."*
>
> – Margaret Mead

As creeks go, Pigeon Creek in Washington State is small potatoes. A web of rivers, creeks and streams drain Washington's famously wet western half, and Pigeon Creek flows barely two miles, dropping 400 feet from its source to Port Gardner Bay on Puget Sound.

Over its lifetime it has cut a considerable ravine in its forested watershed, but with industrialization the trees were logged, the land settled and the creek habitat fouled. Wildlife that had made the creek's waters home fled as the fragile ecosystem collapsed. Recently, however, school children and concerned citizens have worked to restore it, inspiring hope that the creek's rich natural community and its human neighbors can live together in greater harmony.

Near this creek's source a cluster of apartments and offices seeks to inspire another kind of hope. This is Housing Hope Village, one of the many complexes built by Housing Hope, a nonprofit organization founded to provide safe, decent, affordable housing for homeless people and the services required to restore them to economic and civic well-being. With modernization, a habitat that supported human societies for thousands of years was transformed; the immigrant population soared, and immensely powerful social and economic currents altered the very shape of living itself. But for all its power, the complex new world these currents produced proved fragile, and as parts fractured or collapsed, individuals and families found themselves exiled from its promise. Many became homeless in their own land. And as their numbers grew the problems they represented seemed insurmountable.

For the past twenty-five years Housing Hope has demonstrated its ability to address the needs of the homeless successfully and, more significantly, has demonstrated that the problem of homelessness itself can be solved. Because of the scale of the problem and its ramifications, solutions are necessarily varied, complex and far more complicated than restoring a watershed. Housing Hope has restricted its work primarily to one county, but the results it has achieved show that the solutions it crafted work. The effort is worthy of study, and that is the focus of this story.

That county, Snohomish County, describes a rough rectangle of land covering a little more than 2,000 square miles reaching east from Puget Sound, a long arm of the Pacific Ocean, to the crest of the Cascade Mountains. It has been home to human beings for thousands of years, but its recorded history can be measured in just three lifetimes. In 1792, the British naval explorer George Vancouver anchored his ship Discovery near the mouth of the Snohomish River and claimed the land for Great Britain, naming the immediate waters Possession Sound. Half a century later the United States took full possession of the Oregon Territory south of the 49th Parallel. In 1861 the

Washington Territorial legislature carved Snohomish County from Island County, granting articles of incorporation that enabled its commissioners, elected by roughly fifty white American citizens, to levy taxes for improvements.

Only two lifetimes are sufficient to cover the history of Snohomish County's largest city and county seat, Everett, named after the son of Charles Colby. An influential east coast businessman and entrepreneur, the elder Colby convinced his boss, James J. Hill, described by admirers as the Empire Builder, and perhaps more accurately by historian Stewart Holbrook as the "barb-wire, one-eyed old son-of-a-bitch of western railroading," to bring his rail line, the Northern Pacific Railroad, to tidewater on Possession Sound, at Port Gardner Bay in 1893. Colby also convinced John D. Rockefeller to invest in the town site developed there, and their glittering names were sufficient to lure enough local investors to buy into the dream of wealth.

Washington had been a state for only four years when its legislature granted Everett a charter for city government and articles of incorporation similar to those of Snohomish County, providing its administrators authority to tax and issue bonds. But a harbinger of imminent social distress appeared that same year when commissioners erected a poor farm up the river to "Keep, clothe, properly care for and furnish medicine for each of the county paupers at 85 cents a day." Among the initial 26 inmates, as they were termed, were four destitute women.

Everett's stakeholders enjoyed a brief industrial boom preceding a major economic bust. The environmental rapine carried out by the brutal extractive industries of the day initially provided work aplenty but typically produced more timber than an emerging transportation system and national market could absorb, and when glut forced mills to shut down until demand grew again, workers were locked out. As a result the town endured prolonged labor strife that culminated in a bloody massacre in 1916, followed by decades of irregular growth. Yet the dream of its founders survived, emerging from this struggle as a city of smokestacks. The city belched fumes from 12 saw and pulp mills ringing the bay and riverside, spawned a transportation nexus, and became the commercial heart of the county and a complex, cosmopolitan hive of urban activity. By 1960, Everett had ridden the postwar boom to become the county's largest city with more than 40,000 working and middle class citizens proudly supporting schools, churches, hospitals and a thriving downtown. More than a quarter-million inhabitants crowded the county's southwestern quarter in a gaggle of suburban communities dedicated to relentless - but rarely organized - growth. And the boom and bust cycles that marked this city's early economic history continued into the new millennium.

Photo courtesy of Jack O'Donnell

Everett experienced a building boom from 1900-1910

The lumbering, fishing and mining industries of Everett's early economy consumed the labor of a largely transient male population that, thanks to the railroads, arrived when there was work and left when there was not. Such industries were notorious for crushing, dismembering, poisoning and otherwise killing alarming numbers of workers. The injured could seek help from unions and primitive hospital insurance policies, and fraternal groups such as the

Odd Fellows and Masons often paid for burials. Even saloons, everyman's social hall, could be counted on to take up a collection for the destitute widows and orphans, but as the population grew and families put down roots, these informal aids no longer sufficed.

Churches and civic groups were the primary frontier institutions through which community support for charitable action and giving was organized, and out of which systematic efforts to deal with social ills arose. While families could be counted on to take in ill or homeless members, the civic zeal of the Everett Women's Book Club fueled the drive to found Everett General Hospital in 1894 and the city's first public library in 1911. The Roman Catholic Sisters of Providence founded Providence Hospital in 1905, and Methodists took over the county poor farm and sponsored the Deaconess Children's Home in 1911. Everett's Lutherans were also active in developing the town's social institutions, founding the Luther Child Center in 1901 and the short-lived Columbia College in 1909.

Photo courtesy of Jack O'Donnell

Five children pose for a photo outside their Everett home

These familial, social and religious venues developed within the larger economic and civic realities of the United States. Because of Washington's isolation in a far corner of the nation, local action was necessarily collaborative. Heeding public demands for improvements, the state, county and city taxed citizens and issued bonds to develop an infrastructure of roads, schools, water mains and electrical power that promoted economic growth and the general welfare. Working together, private and public bodies addressed problems as they arose. In a population that was primarily rural and agricultural, most families could provide the basic necessities of life for their members, but as the region became more urban and professional, more cooperative planning was required and at a larger scale.

As the population and economy grew apace, concerned citizens called for greater government investment and regulation. Government land grants enabled railroads to span the continent but Congressional action required they publish reasonable rate schedules. As business boomed in the late nineteenth and early twentieth centuries, the Progressive movement sought to restrain the cruel aspects of laissez faire capitalism and unify a vast and turbulent country by extending opportunity to everyone including African Americans, Native Americans and, eventually, women.

Rapid expansion of manufacturing enabled a small group of individuals, families and agencies to amass colossal fortunes, leading critics to brand the captains of industry as robber barons. However, some of the more forward-thinking, or some would say clever, preserved their fortunes by directing assets toward the public good. In Everett, such philanthropy found its clearest expression in U. S. Steel magnate Andrew Carnegie's 1905 gift to the city of $25,000 to house its public library in a grand structure bearing his name. A greater legacy, however, was the professionalization of giving pioneered by the Rockefeller, Ford and other private foundations that hired staffs to survey needs and develop a rational process by which financial grants could be applied for and administered to mediate social ills.

But even greater resources were required to assuage social and economic catastrophe when the precarious financial situation of the late 1920s led to the Wall Street Crash of 1929 and the Great Depression. Few regions were hit harder than western Washington, which still relied on extractive industries like lumbering and fishing, and during the winter of 1932-1933 only 59.1% of Western Washington's production workers were employed. In Everett the mills slumbered. The hard times lasted the better part of a decade and only ended when the world plunged into World War II. During the Great Depression, Snohomish County suffered out-migration and the birth rate declined as marriages were postponed. Families 'doubled-up' to take in the homeless and unemployed. People learned to do without, planted gardens and raised livestock to survive.

Only the federal government was large enough to deal with these calamities, and President Franklin D. Roosevelt's New Deal programs gave people hope and an enduring example of what enlightened, citizen-led government could do. Federal expenditures on huge infrastructure projects like the Bonneville and Grand Coulee Dams and massive military spending during the war created jobs refueling the economy and creating prosperity, just as building the interstate highway system and military spending would keep the economy growing after the war. The memories of privation and terrors of war were, for the most part, subsumed by a rising standard of living, but affluence was tempered by the Cold War and the looming threat of nuclear annihilation.

Now we enter into the modern period, and with greater familiarity and insights from the generations of our grandparents and parents, we can observe how the interactions of forces and events, and the more recent cycles of boom and bust, have brought about the vexing social problems of our own time, similar to those in the past, but different enough to require newer and newly creative solutions. And it is in the character of the founders of Housing Hope that we see how these more recent events made their impression and inspired action.

The Founders of Housing Hope

Amy Youngstrom

Amy Youngstrom

Amy Youngstrom, née Anderson, was born in Olympia, Washington, in 1919, making her the oldest of Housing Hope's founders. Her family had left overpopulated and impoverished Sweden at the turn of the century and farmed briefly in Iowa before heading to the Puget Sound region where their men worked in the woods. By the 1920s, the five Anderson brothers operated mills on Olympia's waterfront, and Ossian Anderson started the Puget Sound Pulp and Timber Co., whose Everett location would be acquired by the Scott Paper Company and later Kimberly Clark. A child of relative affluence, Amy attended Stanford University and the University of Washington's School of Music, married medical student George Youngstrom on Saint Valentine's Day 1942, and graduated with him that June. George served in the Navy during the war, and in 1951 they moved to Mukilteo, southwest of Everett, where he worked as a dermatologist and she contributed to the family's household income by giving piano lessons.

Two of Amy's primary activities were raising four children and serving with her congregation at Everett's First Presbyterian Church, an imposing edifice across the street from the county courthouse. There she joined Church Women United, an ecumenical Christian women's group involved with social justice issues. She also worked with Planned Parenthood, the Everett Food Bank, the Laubach tutoring program for functionally illiterate adults and the American Field Service student exchange program. Living a comfortable, energetic life and supporting the arts, after her children, she devoted herself primarily to serving the needy. Inspired by faith and sustained by a joyful, giving nature and an innate intelligence, she possessed the unique ability to merge the agendas of various groups so that they could work more effectively together. It was only natural, then, when several churches in north Snohomish county elected to work together to solve social problems afflicting the poor in her community, that she would join the effort.

Mae Stork

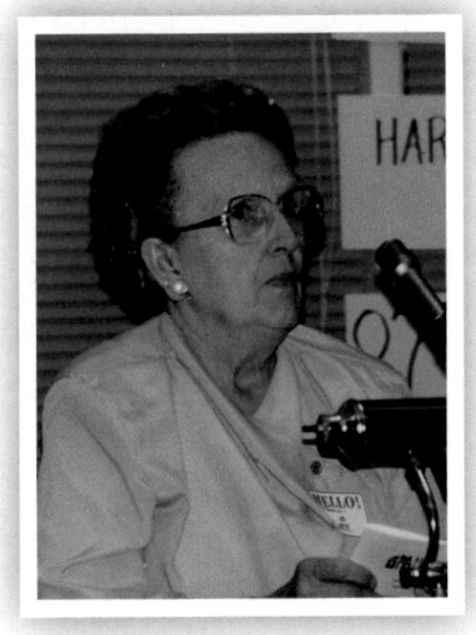

Mae Stork

After three successive summer storms destroyed the crops on their Minnesota farm and hail on the week of July 4th, 1932 flattened one more crop. Edwin "Odie" Erickson and his wife Anna Marjorie piled twelve year-old daughter, Mae, and her younger brother into the old family Ford, tied their possessions on the outside and headed west. Somewhere on a road in the Montana Rockies, the car hit a rut so hard the glass washboard tied to the door shattered. It had been her mother's prized possession; Mae remembered no harsh words but her family drove for miles in silence. Descendents of Swedish pioneers, they headed to Everett where they had kin. They spent the '30s working when they could, spending summers picking fruit in the Yakima Valley, all of them living in a tent. Mae had one dress she wore to school that her mother washed and ironed every night. Odie went to work for the Everett Water Department and, eventually, the family saved enough to purchase a house of their own in north Everett.

In those days, buying a home was a cooperative affair. Well-known Everett real estate developers like Dan Duryee or Steve Saunders sold lots for $400 to $500, about half a worker's annual wage, and worked with local banks that offered loans for lumber and supplies. The buyer might start small with a building that would eventually become a garage, and once this was ready the family could move in and begin housekeeping as the rest of the house took shape. It took time and labor (the modern term is 'sweat equity') but the pride of building and owning a home meant that few loans defaulted. Anna loved her home, and when Mae and her siblings saw other families going camping with their children and asked if they could too, mother said no; she had no desire to camp out ever again. In 1940 Mae married George Stork, who worked for Great Northern, and they began a family of their own.

George Stork's career with the Railroad ended with a back injury, and shortly thereafter his hearing began to fail. Mae supported the family by working in sales for the Goldfinch Bros. Paint Co., and later at Value Mart, but she never felt comfortable in the commercial world with its emphasis on the bottom line. Her daughter, Mayre, described her as having 'a servant's heart,' dedicated to caring. She found inspiration in the social mission of First United Methodist Church on Colby Avenue just south of the city center. George lived at a time when debilities such as his marked one as less of a person and as his deafness grew worse and he could communicate only in writing, he became anxious and depressed. In 1971, on the advice of doctors, the family decided to have him evaluated at Northern State Mental Hospital. At that time, however, free evaluations were only done as part of criminal proceedings. For this to happen, unexpectedly, he was taken into custody by the county sheriff who handcuffed him and kept him for a night in a jail cell with only a stool to sit on before he was taken to the hospital the next day. Unable to understand what was happening, he cried out to his family, "Why did you have me arrested?" and his pain lacerated their souls. In Mayre's words, the indignity 'set my Mom on fire,' and she dedicated herself to work with lobbyists and state legislators for the passage of the Senior Citizens Services Act, so that other families would not have to suffer what hers did. To honor her leadership, Governor Booth Gardiner had her join him in the photograph celebrating its passage in 1976. In the early 1980s, she was very active in her church's social action committee working for the poor with mental difficulties.

Ed Petersen

Ed Petersen

Oyvind Petersen's family endured the Nazi occupation of their native Norway while his father Sigmund was at sea. As a Norwegian seaman, Sigmund faced 2 year assignments away from home, even when he returned to Norway after five years in 1945. So in 1948 he brought his family to the United States, to Everett, where his wife, Bergljiot, or Betty as she was called in America, had kin. Fluent in English because of his travels, he got a job with a tug and barge company that kept him closer to home, and his family started in a modest bayside house across the street from Providence Hospital and then moved to the Riverside area. Oyvind's name was partially Americanized to Ivind and then at age seven to Edwin, or 'Ed'. But Ed, the middle child, grew up feeling embarrassed by his mother's devotion to Norwegian traditions, and that their meals were not at all like what other families ate. From an early age he knew the uncomfortable feeling of being different, which led to a social sensitivity and later an interest in social justice.

Ed was fourteen years old when John Kennedy became President and called for the creation of the Peace Corps. At his family's church, Central Lutheran, he felt at once embraced by the community and challenged by its theology. Through the media he watched the demise of colonialism, the dawn of the space age and the tumult of the civil rights movement. Encouraged by the social gospel he heard preached, he resonated to the calls for social justice for the poor and oppressed here and abroad and was frustrated by the slow recognition in the United States of the evils of segregation and widespread poverty. He wanted to get involved. Inspired by idealism and faith, Ed enrolled at Tacoma's Pacific Lutheran University.

Between two-week voyages, his father purchased apartment houses in the Everett area, and he hoped that one of his sons would someday work with him on these properties. Ed decided to pursue a degree in Business Administration which his father hoped would help him manage the properties, but during his junior year, a sociology class fired his zeal.

He enrolled in the University of Pennsylvania's Master of Social Work program, but this was 1968, at the height of the Vietnam War, and a call from the Everett Draft Board caused a change of plans. Joining the Peace Corps provided a draft deferment. He asked his fiancée, Carol, if she'd join him overseas. They married in August and headed to Venezuela. Before leaving, the clerk at the draft board growled assurance that they'd enroll him upon his return.

CUERPO DE PAZ

EDUARDO PETERSEN
TECNICO DE COOPERATIVAS

OFICINA DEL I. A. N.
CARIPE, MONAGAS

Ed's Peace Corps business card

Todd Morrow

Todd Morrow

Born in 1934, Shirley Morrow's ancestors on her mother's side were Volga German pacifists who left Russia in the latter part of the nineteenth century in part to avoid conscription. They ended up in Nebraska. When Shirley's mother's parents died, Shirley's mom, Dorothy, came west to live with relatives in Everett. Dorothy married WC "Clinton" Briggs and they made their home in Everett to raise Shirley and her two sisters. Everett First Presbyterian Church was a central part of their life. WC became the Chief Engineer at Sumner Iron Works and an elder in the church and was much involved with the Masons and Kiwanis. Dorothy led Presbyterian Women and headed the church's nursery. Shirley followed in her parents' commitment to community and church. For 37 years she worked as a kindergarten teacher while supporting her two sons in their activities, as a Den Mother, band mother and PTA member (she was to earn two Golden Acorn awards). In church she served as a teacher, elder, deacon, and organizer of two vacation church schools. Later, in 2003, Shirley started a weekly free dinner at her church for the needy, called "Dinner at the Bell", so named for the old church bell that stands outside the church entrance where the guests enter for dinner. This effort is still going strong under her leadership and serves delicious home-cooked meals to more than 100 people every Wednesday night. Shirley has never stopped serving, and her love, devotion and generosity inspired both boys.

Today Shirley's younger son Todd Morrow lives just ten blocks from his mother's home in the View Ridge neighborhood, a true son of Everett. Born in 1961, he became an Eagle Scout and thrived in Everett's schools where, during his senior year, he was voted most likely to succeed. He went on to graduate from Stanford University in 1984, and the University of Washington Law School three years later. In his first job clerking for Evergreen Legal Services he provided legal aid for senior assistance programs and canvassed publically owned buildings to inform tenants about their legal rights. His first experience as a trial lawyer came at the trial of his brother, Scott, a founder of Seattle Housing and Resource Effort (SHARE) in 1990. Combined with the Woman's Housing Equality and Enhancement League, SHARE/WHEEL sponsored tent cities throughout King County that were governed by the homeless themselves, and it was during a demonstration to preserve housing that he had been arrested. Scott's idealism inspired the judge's own parents to attend his trial. Even if the self-deprecating answer to the perennial question about the progress of one's children - "at least they aren't in jail" - was only just barely true, Shirley remained immensely proud of her boys and happy to volunteer them on behalf of justice.

Bruce Eklund

Bruce Eklund

Born in Seattle in 1947, Bruce Eklund moved with his family to Spokane and Boise, and followed his older brother to Pacific Lutheran University becoming Ed Petersen's roommate in his junior year. His college years proved the most formative of his life, and the experience of teaching inner city youth as a member of the United Students Social Action Committee sensitized him to the needs of the urban poor. At PLU he met Barbara Maier, whom he married shortly after graduation. While attending seminary for one quarter, it was revealed to him that he would not be able to specialize in youth ministry. He quit. The luckiest draft lottery number of 365 enabled Bruce to return to Oregon for teaching credentials. Teaching alongside Barbara seemed far more attractive, and they enrolled at the University of Oregon to become certificated. An interesting education course in juvenile corrections at the University, then a part-time job working at the Skipworth Juvenile Home, administered by the Lane County Juvenile Court, ignited Bruce's interest in juvenile justice.

The director at Skipworth ran a very effective and progressive program that served its clients well and exposed Bruce to a philosophy he embraced. In 1974, he earned an Interdisciplinary Studies Master's Degree in Juvenile Corrections at the University of Oregon, then applied for and got a job as a probation officer at the Snohomish County Juvenile Court in Everett. He and Barbara moved to Everett where they became members at Our Savior's Lutheran Church. Barbara taught at the Everett Alternative High Everett and became a Reading Specialist for the Everett School District; Bruce's degree enabled him to become the Juvenile Detention Supervisor, where he built on the philosophy modeled at Skipworth. In the early 1980s, Bruce helped organize and then supervised the second Volunteer Guardian ad Litem program in the country, which provided special legal advocacy for children who experienced physical or sexual abuse or neglect. In 1983 he joined with Snohomish County Prosecuting Attorney, Seth Dawson, friends Bill France and Steve Burr and others to start the Open Door Theater, an applied theater program whose presentations in schools helped children at risk of sexual abuse become aware of safety rules including how to seek help. Upon Ed's return to Everett in 1980, the two continued their close relationship.

Jon Witte

Jon Witte

Jon Witte was born in Wausau, Wisconsin into a family of Lutheran "preachers and teachers". While still a young boy, the family moved to Aurora, Illinois where his father taught in a Lutheran elementary school. They lived in a modest home near the church and school where life revolved around faith and community. When Jon was seven years old, his father died of congestive heart failure. His mother, Dorothy, a strong and stoic woman of German descent, had known hard times. She had grown up on a farm in the middle of Kansas, and as the eldest of her siblings, was used to hard work and making ends meet. Knowing she would need to go back to work after her husband's untimely death to support her family, she earned a "woman teacher's salary", less than that of a man's, and they often did without. Yet in the midst of their financial difficulties, church members rallied around Dorothy, and her young family felt cared for by this larger community. As he grew up, Jon intended to follow his parents into a career in teaching, and graduated in 1972 from Concordia Teacher's College in River Forest, Illinois. But in graduate school his plans took an unexpected turn when an advisor encouraged him to apply to medical school. He was accepted to the University Of Illinois School Of Medicine, graduating in 1977. His medical career brought him to Everett in 1982 as a Rheumatologist at the Everett Clinic. Jon and his wife, Donna, had visited the Pacific Northwest on vacations and were thrilled to settle here. They immediately became involved in local political activism and social justice issues and started a family. Meeting Ed and Carol Petersen at Central Lutheran Church and hearing of Ed's ideas to address homelessness in Everett, Jon was reminded of his childhood struggles and of how the community supported his family in a time of need. He wanted to help others just has he had been helped, and becoming involved with Housing Hope beckoned as a means to do this.

These individuals are alike in significant ways. None lived sheltered lives. Most either knew poverty or had vivid enough family histories of it to prevent them from harboring sentimental notions about it, and all had worked with the poor or the distressed. All respected the value of education and had a keen work ethic. All were strongly involved in their churches and participated in their social missions. In Protestant theology doing good to others and serving those in need is seen not so much as a response to a commandment but a thank offering given in spontaneous gratitude for the gift of grace. This tradition played a profound role in the motivation of these individuals, and since the majority of them came from Scandinavian background, we should not dismiss the value of their ethnic heritage. Most emigrants did not leave Norway and Sweden to escape religious persecution or political oppression but because their homelands were unable to feed the growing numbers of their people. Most left with extended families intact, with kin on both sides of the ocean. The sense of personal responsibility nourished by large families remains the bedrock of a civic-mindedness found in Scandinavian culture at home and in America. They also shared a strong commercial sense that had been a hallmark of Scandinavian emigrants, whether they wore horned helmets and swung battle axes or were dressed in farmers' bib overalls and carried scythes. These characteristics were the foundation of Housing Hope's success.

Everett enjoyed many good years after World War II. The smokestacks belched industriously, but a south wind usually carried the stink away from downtown streets packed with workers, shoppers and businesspeople. Rural dairy cooperatives made good money from their products, and during summer months yellow school buses carried mobs of children to the fields where they could earn a few dollars picking flats of berries. Everett's population more than doubled, and new municipalities such as Lynnwood and Mountlake Terrace sprouted southwest of town. Rural communities grew, suburbs spread, roads were paved, highways and freeways appeared and new companies moved in.

But just as a county poor farm accompanied the incorporation of Everett, the post-war boom generated its own inequities. America's affluence was based on manufacturing, but as overseas economies expanded, these jobs were replaced by service sector jobs that tended to pay less. By the 1970s average income stagnated, but as more women entered the workforce families were able to maintain the affluent life styles they had come to enjoy. Food and clothing costs continued their historic declines as a percentage of income, but housing did not, and by the 1980s the continued increase in Snohomish County's population and the decrease of available land led to a sharp rise in housing costs.

With the advent of freeways and cheap air travel Americans became more mobile. The disintegration of familial webs during the Great Depression and World War II, followed by the pattern of post-war suburban growth, eliminated many of the traditional ways people had weathered economic troubles. Moreover, jobs in lumber, fishing, agriculture and manufacturing were replaced by increasingly technical jobs, meaning that an entire echelon of labor - individuals without a high school diploma who had once been the backbone of the national economy - could no longer look forward to a career or even economic security. Among young people, the pervasive sense of anxiety generated by the fear of nuclear catastrophe in the 1950s was exacerbated by the social upheaval and political violence in the '60s. The increasing use of alcohol and drugs in the '70s and '80s were symptomatic of a growing sense that things were not going to improve. As Snohomish County's economy continued to expand during these years, and in-migration approached a flood, homelessness - something not seen in great numbers since the Great Depression - began to show up on the socio-economic radar.

More about Ed

All of the founders introduced thus far agree that Ed Petersen, who has been Housing Hope's Executive Director since its inception in 1987, has been its dominant figure and a major mover in their lives. It is not uncommon for many staff to tear up when they speak about him, and if he is embarrassed by this, he is nonetheless forthright about his abilities. Although he would deny it, Housing Hope is largely his creation, and to understand this and how he corralled all these people into his vision, we need to examine his personal history more closely.

Irrigation pump, Ed and co-op members

Peace Corps Venezuela fostered three varieties of cooperatives: savings and loan, consumer, and agricultural. Many of the 40 volunteers of Ed and Carol's Peace Corps group focused on agricultural co-ops. During training they studied the Rochdale Principles of Cooperative, a program of cooperative formation originating in early nineteenth-century England. Seven principles emphasized the voluntary, democratic, equitable and autonomous nature of successful cooperatives and how they survive by fostering education and training within a web of similar associations embedded in the larger community.

Ed's leadership abilities were apparent at PLU when he was elected president of his service fraternity in his sophomore year and vice president of the student body in his junior year. When he and Carol were sent to the village of La Guanota in eastern Venezuela's Caripe Valley, he developed a knack for community organizing. The rich limestone soil of the mountain valley and its salubrious climate encouraged agriculture, but initially none of the farmers wanted to join a vegetable-growing cooperative. But six months of cajoling and the example set by the two convinced nine individuals to found La Cooperativa El Páramo and apply for a land grant. In response to a petition Ed organized, the Venezuelan government provided 30 hectares of land, built roads and provided irrigation equipment. The co-op started growing vegetables and eventually secured a bank loan to import seed potatoes from Canada. Because the crop was not ready for harvest when Ed and Carol's two years of service were up, they signed on for another year to help the cooperative harvest and obtain a fair price for their produce. But six months into their second year, Carol learned she was pregnant, and because there were no suitable medical facilities nearby, they decided to return to Everett.

The Everett draft board gloated. Ed's Selective Service lottery number, 126, meant the game was up, but he gained another deferment by enrolling in the Pacific Lutheran Theological Seminary at Berkeley, California. During the year he and Carol lived in the Bay Area, he decided that his future lay in secular ministry and he applied again to the University of Pennsylvania. Surprised when the acceptance committee at the School of Social Work turned him down, he did something that was to become a hallmark: he changed their minds.

Politely but effectively he showed them how their decision made no sense: they had accepted him before, and since then he had accumulated many more credentials making him an even more attractive candidate. They agreed, but exercised their prerogative of denying him a scholarship. So, penniless and with

Ed Petersen during Peace Corps days

Carol Petersen with Guaco, their bird

their baby daughter Kim in tow, they spent August of 1972 driving across the country in a Chevy Vega and settling into Philadelphia. While Carol found employment as a hospital social worker, an academic practicum took Ed to nearby Graterford Prison, the largest maximum security prison in Pennsylvania, to develop an inmate educational release program. Impressed by his abilities, the prison superintendent invited him to lead a new program at the Norristown State Hospital, an active psychiatric hospital outside of Philadelphia, where psychotic or suicidal inmates from seven Pennsylvania prisons would be sent for incarcerated therapy. This took place in a 19-unit ward at a maximum security forensic psychiatric facility where security guards and psychiatric security aides from the state mental health system accompanied inmates at all times.

Ed and Carol shared a house with Jeff and Debbie Schein. Jeff was a rabbinical student writing his dissertation on Lawrence Kolberg's work regarding therapeutic community and its relationship with moral reasoning ability. Long conversations convinced Ed that Kolberg's model could work at Norristown, and he convinced staff to try it. At meetings where every inmate and staff member had a voice, the group discussed rules and privileges in the ward, and all participants helped to deal with rule infractions. Implicit in these discussions was the issue of security versus therapy and, following Kohlberg's approach, the idea was to enhance moral reasoning abilities. Carrots or rewards available through community decision making process were special job assignments, greater freedom inside the ward and the ability to go out onto the hospital's bucolic 225-acre grounds. Inmates came to Norristown because they were psychotic, schizophrenic or severely depressed in prison. Individuals had typically suffered severe traumas. The prison's job was to protect society by locking these people up, but Ed's group offered a middle ground. During the two years he worked with them, the inmates consistently wanted to participate, and staff regarded working with his group as the most desirable job in the hospital. With help, Ed had created a unique therapeutic community that worked.

Those who know Ed and Carol well would not be surprised to learn that Ed and Carol planned their life paths. The first ten years of married life was devoted to traveling the world and securing professional degrees. In the spring of '76 Ed traveled to Norway to petition for jobs in six of the nation's Socialskole or professional social schools. But these organizations typically hired Norwegian residents, so they came back to Philadelphia and, in September, returned to the Northwest to look for work. In October, however, the University of Trondheim called. It was starting an advanced program in Social Work and needed professionals with master's degrees, which were not common in Norway. Since Ed had a master's and already spoke Norwegian he was recruited as an Associate Professor of Social Work position for two years. Research was expected and, capitalizing on his experience at Graterford and Norristown, he petitioned Norway's Department of Corrections for a grant to study offender halfway houses in Oslo and Stavanger. By 1979 the ten years were up. A second daughter, Solveig, had been born in Philadelphia, a third daughter, Sonja, in Trondheim, and they were on schedule to come back to the Northwest to settle down.

Ed and Carol retained strong connections with their Lutheran communities, and a brother-in-law in Olympia connected him with a parishioner who was an administrator at the State Parole Board. Because of his research in Norway and prior corrections experience, Ed was hired in 1979 as an administrator for the final phase of a study on determinate and indeterminate sentencing: situations where inmates either do their time in cells or come under the purview of an officer who can alter their penal settings to facilitate a return to society. He and Carol purchased a house in Olympia, but Everett was home, and, on the lookout for job opportunities, he applied at Mental Health Services, Inc. (MHS). The Center's leadership was in transition, and his proposal to create a position as Director of Adult Services made such sense that they hired him to carry it out. By 1980 the Olympia house was sold and they moved to Everett to buy a house near his parents' home.

Mental Health Services (MHS)

MHS (now Compass Health) was organized in 1971 to provide services for patients with mental health issues living in Everett and Snohomish County, part of a national movement away from housing mental patients in large asylums and toward a more community-based approach. Greater understanding of mental illness, the development of psychotropic drugs, and a litany of horror stories about large institutions persuaded many that this was a more humane approach, but budget cuts became the major driver of the process. In 1973, the Northern State Hospital in Sedro-Woolley, in Skagit County (just north of Snohomish County), was closed in deference to community-based programs. Upon discharge many residents would become homeless. Many ended up in prison.

Ed endeavored to help adult clients receive services and maintain independent lives, but found that the rock upon which many foundered was the lack of affordable housing. In Everett, a blue-collar working-class town whose citizens took pride in their independence and the ability to take care of their own, there were few opportunities for the homeless without families nearby to find adequate shelter. In 1917, the Snohomish chapter of the American Red Cross had been organized in Everett; among other things, the Red Cross works to provide temporary shelter and help for people made homeless by disasters. In 1931, the Bethany Home at 3322 Broadway Avenue received support from a consortium of Everett churches, enabling it to provide shelter for needy elderly who would otherwise have been homeless and in 1942 Catholic Charities founded the Catholic Children's Bureau in Everett to care for orphans and abandoned children. In 1961 the Everett Gospel Mission had developed a short term shelter in town for homeless men and later for women; other agencies provided vouchers for apartment stays and some agencies staffed food banks, but the problem continued to grow. In the 1980s, Volunteers of America (VOA), a national Christian charity, built a Community Resource Center on north Broadway in Everett where it provided food, shelter services, skills training and dispute resolution to low income families and the homeless.

A relatively small tax base presented a challenge for the city and county to support these services and safety net programs, much less provide affordable housing. In larger communities such as Seattle, nonprofits like the Fremont Public Association and the Capitol Hill Housing Improvement Program had been providing housing since the 1960s, but there were no such programs in Snohomish County. MHS began seeking affordable housing solutions for mentally ill individuals, and in this capacity Ed met Mae Stork.

As a member of her church's social action committee, Mae had made contact with several poor individuals with mental difficulties and was trying to find them better services. Having contacted Ed, she invited him to go with her to meet one of her clients, a young man named Daniel who lived in a dismal apartment in Everett. With Ed's help, she was able to improve Daniel's situation. Ed and Mae shared concerns about the difficulties the mentally ill faced who were homeless or threatened with homelessness. Old enough to be Ed's mother, her energy and determination to serve when many her age would be working on their bridge game made a deep impression on him.

As Ed and Mae's congregations strove to address the area's pressing social problems, it became obvious that their scale and complexity prevented any one congregation from doing more than treating symptoms. Homelessness had become a common feature, and in conversations with Bruce Eklund, his old friend from college days, the three discussed its impact on youth as well as mental patients. Even more alarming, in addition to itinerant transients and hobos on the lower rung of the working class, local pastors found that more and more of the homeless families showing up at their doorsteps asking for help included children. Workable solutions were needed, but to even begin down this road, the churches would have to work together. Earlier attempts to develop ecumenical ministries had come to naught, and there was no effective ministerial association in the county to coordinate their energies.

The North Snohomish County Association of Churches (NSCAC)

During the time these issues were becoming prominent Chris Boerger and Mark Samuelson were co-pastors at Central Lutheran. Mark's ancestors had been Norwegian pioneers in North Dakota, and he came from a long line of ministers in the

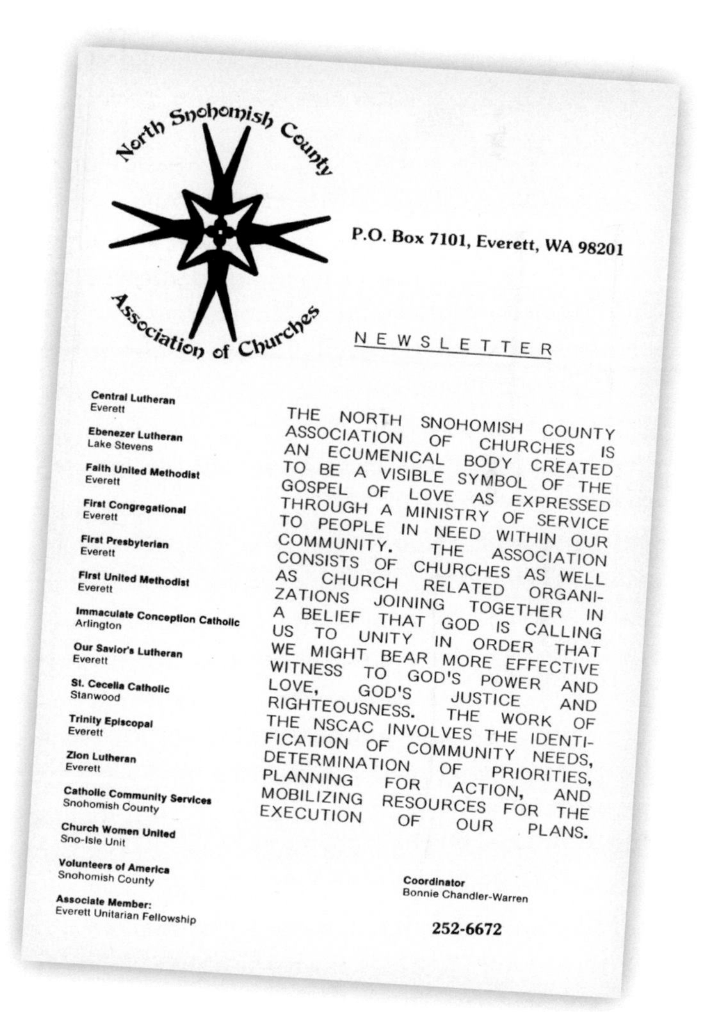

North Snohomish County Association of Churches

P.O. Box 7101, Everett, WA 98201

NEWSLETTER

Central Lutheran
Everett

Ebenezer Lutheran
Lake Stevens

Faith United Methodist
Everett

First Congregational
Everett

First Presbyterian
Everett

First United Methodist
Everett

Immaculate Conception Catholic
Arlington

Our Savior's Lutheran
Everett

St. Cecelia Catholic
Stanwood

Trinity Episcopal
Everett

Zion Lutheran
Everett

Catholic Community Services
Snohomish County

Church Women United
Sno-Isle Unit

Volunteers of America
Snohomish County

Associate Member:
Everett Unitarian Fellowship

THE NORTH SNOHOMISH COUNTY ASSOCIATION OF CHURCHES IS AN ECUMENICAL BODY CREATED TO BE A VISIBLE SYMBOL OF THE GOSPEL OF LOVE AS EXPRESSED THROUGH A MINISTRY OF SERVICE TO PEOPLE IN NEED WITHIN OUR COMMUNITY. THE ASSOCIATION CONSISTS OF CHURCHES AS WELL AS CHURCH RELATED ORGANIZATIONS JOINING TOGETHER IN A BELIEF THAT GOD IS CALLING US TO UNITY IN ORDER THAT WE MIGHT BEAR MORE EFFECTIVE WITNESS TO GOD'S POWER AND LOVE, GOD'S JUSTICE AND RIGHTEOUSNESS. THE WORK OF THE NSCAC INVOLVES THE IDENTIFICATION OF COMMUNITY NEEDS, DETERMINATION OF PRIORITIES, PLANNING FOR ACTION, AND MOBILIZING RESOURCES FOR THE EXECUTION OF OUR PLANS.

Coordinator
Bonnie Chandler-Warren

252-6672

NSCAC newsletter

American Lutheran Church, the more liberal branch of North American Lutheranism. Central Lutheran was his second pastorate and he had charge of the social mission of the church. In the late '70s many churches involved themselves in the work of resettling Southeast Asian refugees, a tragic human wreckage of America's disastrous war in Vietnam. One of the more effective parishioners in this effort was Elizabeth Sipe, a remarkably skillful woman who made contacts, elicited support, developed programs and scared up enough supplies and housing to resettle scores of families - but in a way that did not alienate those who would otherwise have been naysayers. In fact, she inspired one such individual to organize a potluck gathering at Lake Stevens in the early '80s that eventually succeeded in providing housing for 50 Cambodian refugees. Mark noticed that Ed was very impressed by her abilities and the results achieved.

Ed described himself and Carol and Jon and Donna Witte as social justice rabble-rousers in their adult Sunday school classes at Central Lutheran, and Bruce and Barbara raised the same ruckus at Our Savior's. Mark Samuelson still has vivid, fond memories of a series of classes where thoughts caught fire, the right questions were asked and a feeling of group resolve was palpable. Bruce recalls that Ed was chomping at the bit to do something more than what he was doing at MHS, to become invested in something that would create a palpable change. Instead of mitigating local social problems, could the churches solve them by working together? Throughout the following year Mark recalls that Ed employed his celebrated networking skills by connecting with Mae Stork at First Methodist, Amy Youngstrom and Shirley Morrow at First Presbyterian, and Barb Stave and Anita Olson at Our Saviors Lutheran to realize a vision. In January 1984, during the week of Epiphany, commemorating the holy family's bringing their child to the temple for circumcision, to be marked as an offering to God and a blessing to the people, the pastors and representatives from First Presbyterian, from the two Lutheran churches and those from First United Methodist, Trinity Episcopal, First Congregational and Immaculate Conception Catholic Church (from Arlington) met in the basement of St. Paul's Methodist Church, drew their folding chairs into a circle and created a united body that would try.

Out of this came the North Snohomish County Association of Churches (NSCAC), today's Interfaith Association of Northwest Washington. Its executive board of nine members and officers met monthly, supervised by a board of representatives from each congregation that met annually. Articles of Incorporation were submitted to the State and 501(c)3 status sought from the IRS to recognize them as a nonprofit charitable organization. All Executive Board members were non-paid volunteers, including Ed, elected as President with the mission to serve the poor, homeless and hungry of Snohomish County.

To educate themselves and their constituents the NSCAC hosted annual forums examining social problems. They invited speakers, including Ed who presented a workshop on homelessness and Bruce Eklund who presented one on child abuse prevention and juvenile justice. To highlight the problem of hunger the Association contracted with the Church World Service (CWS) out of Miami, Florida. When it was founded in 1946, CWS announced its intention, in a gush of postwar idealism, to eliminate world hunger and poverty and promote peace and justice, and in the 1960s began its largest fundraising effort by promoting Christian Rural Overseas Program (CROP) hunger walks, during which participants raised funds by soliciting pledges for miles walked, in communities throughout the country. NSCAC and CWS brought the CROP walks to Snohomish County. Most of the funds pledged for these walks went to overseas aid groups, but up to 25% stayed in the local community to support local food banks and community gardens. CROP walks organized by Amy Youngstrom and others proved to be one of NSCAC's most popular activities.

It is useful to remember that these were the years when the New Federalism of the Reagan administration made a major effort to increase the influence of state

Crop Walk with Everett
Mayor Bill Moore

governments and reduce what conservative theorists judged the intrusive and counterproductive influence of the federal government. The consolidation of federal expenditures for social programs and their replacement with block grants administered by the states helped bring about the change.

A large tax cut further reduced the federal ability to fund programs such as the Comprehensive Employment and Training Act that provided jobs to low income workers and the long term unemployed. Administering and maintaining social programs increasingly became the responsibility of the states, but the loss of 60,000 high-paying jobs in Washington State when the Boeing Corporation lost federal funding for the supersonic transport, along with other similar downturns, resulted in a severe local recession. The state used much of its block grant funding to maintain weakened programs and shifted its focus from large cities to suburban and rural areas. The result of this and a six-hundred-million-dollar cut in the state's Department of Social and Health Services budget was that services to the poor were crippled, especially in urban areas. As Snohomish County's economy began to rebound in the early '80s, an influx of population produced a housing shortage and an increase in rents. In that decade, federal funding for low income housing plunged 70%, and by the mid '80s, the homeless were camping out under freeway overpasses and in encampments along the river. In 1987, 44% of the county's homeless families had been made so by evictions when they could no longer pay rent. More and more found themselves moving in with relatives and friends, living in cars, or camping out in parking lots and state parks.

The Growing Problem of Homelessness

In 1985, County Executive Willis Tucker appointed Ed to a Homelessness Task Force that examined the nature and extent of homelessness in the county. Since developers had few tools in their kits for low-income housing, they focused on building houses for those who could pay market prices and as a result the rise in housing prices exacerbated the problem of homelessness. In response the county developed a strategy called 'green tagging' that streamlined the permit process, cutting time and costs for the construction of low-income housing. Even so, the task force would note that more than 18,000 renter households in the county earned less than 50% of the state median income and spent more than 30% of their income on rent and utilities. To deal with this problem the NSCAC formed a committee to find solutions and, Ed recruited Shirley Morrow to be in charge of the committee.

Part of the work of the Task Force was to survey agencies serving the homeless. Everett Gospel Mission, the largest shelter in the county, split up homeless families by sheltering men and boys in one facility and women and children in another. After several days of gratis shelter, it charged a nominal rent of $5 a night if clients were able to pay. Other agencies offered emergency shelter vouchers for homeless families to get a room at a motel for up to three nights. Data showed that 55% of those seeking shelter were homeless families. In 1987, 548 homeless families - 3,540 individuals including 919 children - sought refuge at Snohomish County shelters for a total of 47,290 'bed-nights,' a dolorous term identifying one person in one bed for one night. Of these, 61% testified that high rents were their biggest obstacle to finding shelter. Another 2,600 requests for shelter were denied due to lack of beds - a 78% increase over 1986. The County estimated that 27,904 households qualified for federal housing assistance, but there were only 4,904 subsidized low-income housing units in the county. Nationally, the data was equally grim. On any given night approximately 735,000 individuals - 100,000 of them children - had no home in which to sleep. The count of homeless children on the streets began to outnumber the usual crowd of alcoholics and former mental patients - and this number only accounted for those from intact families, leaving out the run-away, throw-away or otherwise abandoned children. In its April 4, 1989 issue, the *Everett Herald* quoted writer and activist Jonathan Kozol in his book, *Rachel and Her Children: Homeless Families in America*: "Shelters are becoming the low-income housing of the 1980s. They represent, in fact, one of the few growth areas in housing for poor people. The other area of growth is prisons." In an ABC television interview, news commentator David Brinkley grimly reported that in 1985, 1,010 homeless Americans died of exposure to cold, far more than had succumbed a decade earlier. In 1988, in Seattle alone, 110 homeless adults died on the streets.

Three years earlier, in 1985 in Everett, Bill Little, the unofficial mayor of 'Trails End,' a nearby homeless encampment on the bank of the Snohomish River, had been shot dead while urinating on the flower garden of a neighborhood property owner. The stark presence of the homeless in downtown Everett and their aura of criminality caused several in the business community to complain that the homeless were scaring customers and businesses away. One Herald reporter quoted a city councilman's suggestion that the homeless be given plastic trash bags and told to clean the streets. These could be swapped for a bowl of soup, a sandwich and a bus ticket to another city, so the city could, in his words, "ship 'em off to someplace else." Another councilman complained that the city shouldn't be in the 'hotel business.' The mayor proposed luring the

Help the homeless sign from an NSCAC event

homeless away from downtown to a transient day center where they could shower, do their laundry, get counseling, and have at least one meal and a place to sleep. "It's like putting sugar out for flies: you are going to get a bunch of them."

Shirley Morrow's NSCAC committee built on her son Scott's work with homeless encampments by highlighting the ease with which landlords evicted tenants and the difficulties this imposed on those who were already struggling. The housing shortage motivated landlords to raise rents, and the task force learned that landlords could do so virtually without restraint. In addition to losing shelter, the evicted also lost their addresses, making it virtually impossible to apply for work or aid or receive mailed checks. Working with the Snohomish County Alliance to End Homelessness, a group planning a future bond or levy for low-income housing, committee members crafted a measure requiring landlords to issue just-cause eviction notices prior to taking action against tenants. The Alliance also helped 37 ministers form a lobbying group, Clergy for Affordable Housing, to raise this issue at the local and state level. In early 1985, Central Lutheran donated $1,500, not an inconsiderable sum for them, to the NSCAC in hopes that it could somehow deal with the issue of family homelessness and not just its symptoms. But the need for emergency housing was great, and the money bought little more than vouchers for bed-nights in motels.

That $1,500 was gone in a week. The NSCAC executive board was shocked. A few families had been sheltered for a few days and then were back out on the street. What had been accomplished aside from supplementing the incomes of motel owners? One could house as many of the homeless as possible, but that would not address the problems that made them homeless in the first place.

The county had already concluded that it needed a housing agency to provide shelter and another agency to address service needs, but in the era of small government, the likelihood of creating such programs shrank, even as the need increased. Indeed, there was mounting fear that continued stringency in the state budget and a huge increase in the federal deficit would cause even sharper declines in subsidies to renters and first-time home buyers. Housing the homeless was a growing local problem needing local solutions devised by local leadership and funded, by default, with local money.

The idea that Mark Samuelson sensed arising in the adult Sunday school took shape during long and detailed conversations. Jon Witte recalled that these brought up memories of his own childhood and he wondered aloud if a program would enable him to help others as he had been helped. Some believed the problem of homelessness was temporary; others feared it would only increase. Temporary or growing, serious efforts to deal with it would require sustained effort, hard work, tough love and the wisdom of serpents. Ed had already written a proposal for a Volunteers In Service To America (VISTA) project, which would work through Mental Health Services to create better housing solutions. Three volunteers would be recruited to help support the establishment of a nonprofit housing agency to produce low-income housing. Mae Stork joined VISTA and became one of the three.

NSCAC members discussed what it would take to deal with the problems faced by the homeless. What was required, as Jon Witte described it, was a profound paradigm shift in thinking about the homeless: away from a 'revolving door' approach and its reliance on emergency housing to one that crafted services that could help those being sheltered. Few homeless had sufficient job skills, and many, debilitated by mental illness, violent home lives, substance abuse, poor education and a numbing history of poverty did not even have the skills to lead independent lives. How could these problems be addressed? Many were single women, with babies and small children, trapped in poverty. How could they be helped to prosper? The idea of a comprehensive program to address these problems had never been considered. What would it look like? Professional case management at emergency shelters might identify the reasons why a person or a family was homeless. Then their needs could be addressed by referring them to agencies offering appropriate services. To the extent that other organizations could provide these, it was agreed that once affordable housing was established the services should be accessed and not duplicated.

Shirley and Todd Morrow, June 1987

Fortunately, Snohomish County and City of Everett agencies had developed convivial collaborative relationships and were not plagued by the turf wars of other counties where agencies fought each other to hold on to clients and funding sources. In order to avoid duplication and serve the groups that needed it most, it was decided to focus on two primary populations: homeless families and mentally ill individuals. A program providing shelter and services would be expensive, it would require complex funding schemes and steady sources of revenue, and it would depend on local support—the civic community would have to be convinced that it worked. To succeed long term, it had to work from the beginning. Shirley Morrow's committee recommended the NSCAC develop a new nonprofit agency to develop low-income housing. It would need a good lawyer, and Shirley volunteered her son Todd, fresh out of law school, who never could say no to his mother.

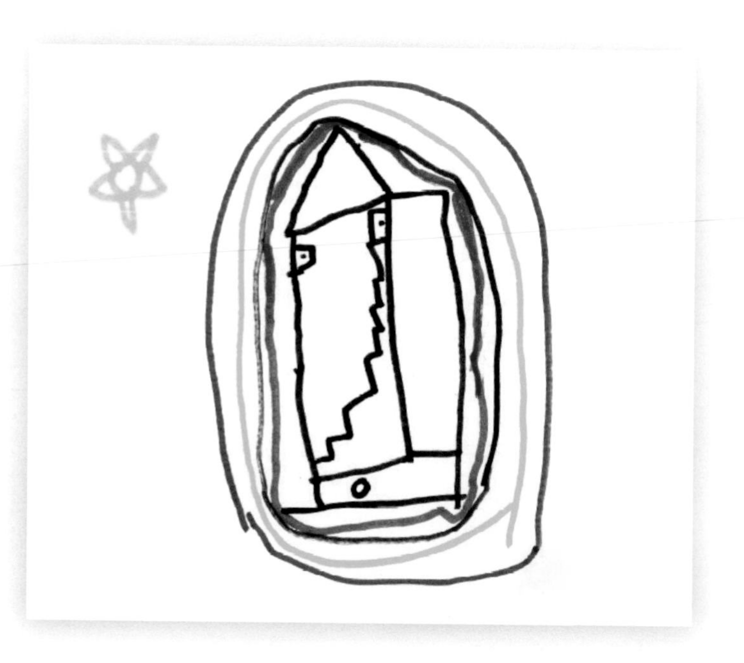

Chapter 2 Vision In Action: 1988-1989

On September 30, 1987, Bruce Eklund, Todd Morrow, Ed Petersen, Mae Stork, Jon Witte and Amy Youngstrom entered the Friendship Room at Central Lutheran and circled the chairs to create the first nonprofit Housing Development Corporation in Snohomish County.

Central Lutheran Church Friendship Room: Site of Housing Hope founding meeting

In choosing the board's officers, Ed asked Amy if she would be president and she agreed, but only on a voluntary basis until a regular president could be elected. Later her husband, George, would explain that by then she had lost any ability to say no to a good cause. Mae was voted vice president; Todd, secretary and Jon treasurer. Bruce said he could volunteer his help for one year. They all agreed that Ed should serve as executive director to carry out the goals set by the board. Todd would draw up articles of incorporation and apply for 501(c)3 status. Ed reviewed the events that had brought them together and summarized a proposed mission statement: ***to promote and provide housing for Snohomish County residents needing assistance, in order to obtain and maintain safe, decent and affordable housing***. The board agreed to submit a proposal for Community Development Block Grant (CDBG) funding and decided to meet, at most, every two weeks. With hope and an opening prayer, a small group of thoughtful, committed citizens set about to change their world.

Less than a week later they were unexpectedly back in the Friendship Room. The NSCAC Executive Committee had recommended that a family emergency shelter be first on a list to receive funds currently available from a Snohomish County Community Services Block Grant (CSBG). However, since no provider had voiced interest in developing a shelter, it was feared that when the CSBG advisory committee met the next day, they might allocate the funds to a different purpose. The board moved, seconded and passed that the newly formed Housing Development Corporation make its voice heard. There was also the issue of a better name for their group. A nominal group process had brainstormed a list of 40 names and solicited gut reactions to them. Housing Hope and Hope Works consistently topped the short list, and these were given to the board for consideration.

At the October 14 meeting, Amy started the discussion, explaining how she and George had gone over the list and personally felt that Housing Hope sounded the best. The board agreed and Housing Hope it became, and Hope Works was remembered

HOUSING CORPORATION

BOARD OF DIRECTORS MEETING
September 30, 1987 Minutes

Present: Amy Youngstrom, Todd Morrow, Mae Stork, Bruce Eklund, Jon Witte, Ed Petersen

ITEM 1: Amy Youngstrom agreed to serve as chairperson until elections take place.

ITEM 2: Todd Morrow agreed to serve as secretary until elections take place.

ITEM #: Ed Petersen reviewed the background for the creation of the Housing Corporation.
A summary of mission statement, goals and possible projects was distributed.

ITEM 4: Ed Petersen was designated as Executive Director.

ITEM 5: The CDBG proposal was discussed. A resolution approving submittal of the proposal was moved, seconded and carried.

ITEM 6: The next two meetings were scheduled for 12:30 p.m. at Central Lutheran Church on October 14 and October 28.

Todd E. Morrow 10/6/87
Todd Morrow, Secretary

First meeting minutes

and used for another nonprofit agency two decades later. They were also told that First Presbyterian's pastor, Dr. Ed Coon, and his congregation had offered $4,500 as seed money for a homeless family shelter, contingent upon Housing Hope securing a site and raising the rest of the money. By this time, Ed, Todd and three others had gone to the Everett City Council and asked Connie Niva, then a councilwoman, to express support for their application for Block Grant funding. The Eklunds had a close relationship with Connie through mutual friends, and the Petersens knew her as well. She was encouraging, and the board approved drafting a proposal requesting $25,000 in City of Everett CDBG funding to acquire property for a Family Emergency Shelter. Ed and the VISTA volunteers had already located a promising site, the eleven-unit MelMar apartment building with an adjoining three bedroom house on Rucker Hill, a prominent neighborhood in Everett.

The city responded favorably, setting aside federal monies for the acquisition. The Everett Housing Authority also advised Housing Hope to apply for rehabilitation funds to bring the 96-year-old building up to code as a serviceable shelter. To keep track of finances, the agency organized its accounting system parallel to one used by United Way. Meanwhile, Amy, Mae and another volunteer, Candy Simon, researched program models for emergency shelters. As fundraising gathered momentum, the agency's bylaws were enacted, additional board members selected and the board scheduled a three-hour workshop on "Essentials for Successful Boards" presented by the United Way of Snohomish County. It was a busy year.

Central to Housing Hope's survival and success was the ethic it nourished from the beginning. Track record was everything—it could survive only if the public believed in it. Fundamental to this ethic was the idea of the double bottom line: that the agency would remain true to its mission of service and also would follow a clear and effective business plan. To gain public support, both were important.

In order for the board to build all aspects of the agency simultaneously, each member agreed to head or serve on key committees and regularly submit ideas to the board for adoption.

They were all volunteers, several working full-time jobs and maintaining families in addition to devoting time to Housing Hope. VISTA volunteers, like their counterparts in the Peace Corps, earned a pittance. Ed worked full time at Mental Health Services, but having convinced his superiors that Housing Hope served their purposes, they agreed to keep paying him his full-time salary as he spent some work hours and his extra hours developing Housing Hope. When office space became necessary, Luther Child Center offered its gym. By Thanksgiving 1987, the State had approved the agency's Articles of Incorporation.

As new people were invited onto the board, mention should be made of several who were instrumental in answering a question all asked: how does a brand new housing agency become successful? Greg Provenzano, the first new board member and an attorney for Evergreen Legal Services, championed serving the lowest income population. There was broad support for this on the board but Ed recalls that no one was as passionate about it as Greg. "He brought the issue forward whenever there was a policy consideration or program being planned. When opportunities for new resources become available, it is easy to migrate to choices that are simpler to implement. Greg always held our feet to the fire to justify decisions and plans against the criteria of serving those in greatest need."

Todd Morrow, Ed, Greg and Rebecca Provenzano

Ron Wilmot of Northcreek Presbyterian brought property acquisition and management know-how to bear; Nik Halladay, a member of First United Methodist, brought property development experience from his work at Pioneer Bank; and Wayne Blakely, a member of Immaculate Conception Catholic Church and a Realtor, organized the agency's Property Development Committee. In Ed's words, their experience and skill opened housing development doors.

By making it a point to include bankers, real estate agents, developers and lawyers on its board, the agency purposely made itself beneficiary to their highly specialized skills. Although they came from many or no religious backgrounds and represented widely divergent political and social views, agreement about need and a preference for knowledgeable, practical solutions helped realize the ideal of the double bottom line. Their passion was as important as their skills and experience.

Ron Wilmot

When Ed delivered the eulogy at Wayne Blakely's Requiem Mass in May 2010, he spoke for them all: "Wayne had this deep commitment and passion for the needs, combined with real estate savvy and creativity. He knew how to talk to sellers, and make them feel good about selling their property for this purpose. He knew how to craft the whole process. Project by project, we did it. We gained the confidence of funders, lenders and donors."

Nik Halladay

Wayne Blakely

Crossroads Emergency Shelter

Jim Wilkinson, a Windermere Realtor, helped Housing Hope negotiate the purchase and sale agreement for the MelMar Apartments on Norton Avenue. To someone unaware of how real estate deals are put together, the finance involved with this project provides a glimpse. Funding entities favor agencies with track records that show broad community support. If many small contributions from local groups could convince a bank to make a loan or a municipal agency to provide a grant, these initial small loans and grants could be used to convince state and federal agencies to make larger loans and grants. This process, called leveraging, uses what one has as a means to generate more so that, as Ed told Connie Niva in their conversations about CDBG funding, each donated dollar could be leveraged to bring in perhaps ten more dollars.

The MelMar building was originally a single-family residence built by Frank Friday in 1892, and later purchased by William Stockbridge, president of Everett's Commerce Bank. The three-bedroom house came later, and in 1927 its owner converted Friday's home into apartments. In 1987, the MelMar was put up for sale. The seller was willing to sell on a real estate contract for $233,000. Backed by the NSCAC and already receiving private donations, Housing Hope was deemed to be viable and was awarded $25,000 in CDBG funds by the city of Everett. Housing Hope used this funding to make a down payment on the apartments and house, leaving a debt of $208,000. Five of the eleven apartments were converted to emergency shelter units. The remaining six apartments and the house were rented out to low-income individuals, providing a stream of rental income that made the monthly debt payment to the seller. Such a seller-financed arrangement, where seller and buyer agree on terms without need of a bank, exemplifies how nonprofits, grantors and sellers work together to leverage smaller amounts, real and projected, from several financing streams to put together a larger package which provides a greater outcome than what the individual amounts could have accomplished on their own. One could describe it as a kind of financial and social gestalt, where a $4,500 commitment from First Presbyterian Church was leveraged into a $233,000 property acquisition that has served homeless families for a quarter century.

Washington's Transient Accommodations law allowed property owners to provide up to two emergency shelter units without a conditional use permit. But the agency planned to shelter five homeless families in its apartments. The city, following its Special Property Use Permit ordinance, required the property owner to give notice to neighbors of the intentions and to arrange a meeting for a public hearing during which neighbors could ask questions and express opinions. Using a community organizing strategy, Housing Hope moved quickly to preempt potential neighborhood opposition to the agency's purchase and its planned programs by sending Mae and her fellow VISTA volunteers door to door handing out information and invitations to a neighborhood meeting. This turned out well enough that the hearing examiner gave them the go-ahead in a 20-page Conditional Use Permit. Regulations triggered other requirements, such as a fire sprinkler system that cost $35,000, an expensive surprise requiring the agency to temporarily reduce the number of emergency shelter units to two in order to buy time to bring the project up to code.

In March of 1988, the agency developed an $88,000 operating budget for the Crossroads Family Emergency Shelter. By late summer of the same year, acquisition of the property was completed, and on August 25 the first families were welcomed into two apartments. September 29th was chosen as the date for the ribbon cutting, which was combined with a celebration of Housing Hope's first anniversary. The Port Gardner neighborhood is an eclectic mix of large, comfortable old craftsmen houses and more humble dwellings. Dowdy and worn out pressed board shingles covered this particular old building, but Housing Hope would remove these and repair the original siding, and it would be painted an attractive forest green. Crossroads would be restored as a handsome—even elegant—addition.

The name Crossroads resonated with the founders' ministry: the struggle to realize social justice. Each participant had traveled their own road to reach this point and the journey they undertook together would be nothing if not challenging. Beginnings are always crossroads where past confronts present to enter the future, and Housing Hope presented itself as a crossroads for its guests, pointing out a hopeful way to a more abundant life. It also served as an example for Snohomish County which needed a successful approach to the homeless problem. Underpinning it all was the hope that the program could attract

Ribbon cutting and grand opening of Crossroads Apartments

the generosity and intelligence of the community to help overcome the problems and shortcomings that it would surely meet along the way.

Family sheltered in 1988

Among Crossroads' early emergency shelter residents was Sheryl Eddy. An Everett native, she had returned in August after two years in Arizona with sons aged three and seven to discover she would need $1,000 to cover the first and last month's rent plus a damage deposit for a local apartment—far more than she had. Desperate, she found her way to Housing Hope which had a place for her at Crossroads, and its staff helped her find a job that she began in November. "Most people come here," Ed Petersen told an Everett Herald reporter, "with a feeling of despair. They can't put a roof over their children's heads. Our task is to rebuild hope…"

A Transition from Shelter: The Housing Continuum

As work went ahead on Norton Avenue, Ed, Amy and the new Property Committee of the board, led by Ron Wilmot, scouted new properties for transitional housing, a term which in 1987 had barely entered the public lexicon. Emergency shelters got people out of their cars or off the streets for 30 days, but what happened to them after that? Mental health workers and staff in correctional facilities observed that many patients released into the community were unable to adapt or cope and ended up back in their institutions. A few halfway houses that provided additional counseling and treatment during a phased re-entry into regular life began appearing in the 1970s. But not until 1986 did the federal government embrace this concept for the homeless, and one year later the McKinney-Vento Homeless Assistance Act granted federal funds to programs that provided transitional housing for the homeless. Ed and Bruce followed this development in their professional work, and on the cutting edge of a new idea, Housing Hope became the first agency in Snohomish County to secure a McKinney grant to provide transitional housing for homeless families.

From the beginning, Housing Hope planned to do more than just put roofs over heads. Some wanted to shelter as many as possible and as soon as possible. If it built a barracks the homeless would surely come, but would they think it home? Would such a place create a stepping-stone to real solutions and nurture the dignity that comes from a sense of accomplishment? To develop a program with housing that would instill pride and where the homeless could be empowered to become self-sufficient was scarcely dreamed of much less realized, at least in Snohomish County. No one had yet figured out how to do this. But transitional housing might provide a way. If it did, it would only be done one family at a time. Housing Hope would learn how to do it in a way that protects and nourishes residents' psyches which have been wounded by circumstance or personal experience. Neighborhoods in which Housing Hope operated its facilities had to be considered; the current members of a neighborhood could all too easily imagine an invasion by ragged, wild-eyed vagrants if the numbers were too large. But just as importantly, the smaller, fragile communities within the facilities themselves had to be considered. To learn how to do this, the agency temporarily leased a triplex from the Red Cross and another five apartments nearby from the Everett Housing Authority, and used them for transitional housing while working to create facilities of its own.

Housing Hope settled on a two-year transitional housing model as a means to stabilize families in distress and assist them towards self-sufficiency. Immediate needs were assessed: health checked, dental work done and referral to treatment for alcohol abuse and drug dependency provided, if needed. And while individuals worked on their General Educational Diploma (GED) attainment or job training or went to appointments, their children would be cared for. Not all applicants would embrace this brisk regimen; poverty does not often inspire an upbeat mood, but for those willing, Housing Hope could offer a hand up. But none of this was going to be cheap.

The first case manager earned $20,000 a year. Her caseload would not exceed 20. Resident managers, hired from among its residents, were given a free or discounted apartment and could earn up to $10 an hour. The success of the program was measured by the success of its residents.

A $1,000 contribution from Everett's First Congregational Church seeded a transitional housing capital fund that the agency used to leverage a CDBG block grant of nearly $70,000 for more transitional housing units. Suitable properties needed more than three units, and half of the units would need to have three or more bedrooms to accommodate large families. Proposals were made for another CDBG grant to fund a second case manager. Over time, Housing Hope hired more case managers and eventually was able to reduce the caseload to a maximum caseload 14. In addition to a case manager and resident manager, in late 1988 the agency hired a part-time office manager and a housing developer.

Aat Bontje, the housing developer, had emigrated from Holland to Canada as a young adult after experiencing the horrors of World War II. Upon earning his Master's of Social Work degree he became a community organizer, teacher and property manager. In 1987 Aat's wife, Pearl Wollin, was working at Providence Hospital in Everett and Ed's wife Carol Petersen was Pearl's social work intern. It was through Carol and Pearl that Aat met Ed and became Housing Hope's first housing developer, working from a beat-up old desk on the Luther Child Center's gym stage.

Aat Bontje, housing developer

He showed a remarkable ability to locate interesting properties in good locations that could be acquired at agreeable prices. During the agency's first decade, Aat found many of the agency's most significant properties, and he was the kind of manager who donned a carpenter's apron and carried out rehabilitation work himself, so he knew if a building was a good investment. He also understood quality workmanship. When he noticed one hired crew carrying rubble out to the dumpster by hand, he asked "Don't you have a wheelbarrow?" "No" came the reply. Aat had Housing Hope purchase a wheelbarrow so the contractor could pick up the pace a bit, suggesting to Ed that in future hires, such slackers be avoided. An early proponent of sustainable practices, over the years he was, with permission, able to salvage much scrap destined for the landfill, to skillfully craft many features in the lovely old home he and Pearl restored in south Everett. In the future this home would from time to time be used to showcase artifacts from Housing Hope's early years.

After an extensive property search, Aat, Ed and the board's property committee found good development prospects in two adjoining lots, both with large frame houses, just a block away from Crossroads and an empty church ideal for redevelopment on Harrison Avenue in Everett's riverside neighborhood.

A three-step housing continuum approach program took shape. Providing families with emergency shelter was the first step; providing transitional housing to give them 'a hand up, not a hand out' was a second. Case managers in both programs helped residents identify the problems they faced and provided or pointed them toward the services they needed. Finally, low-income apartments could provide affordable permanent housing for those graduating from transitional housing into self-sufficient lives. These became the three pillars of what Housing Hope described as its service-enriched housing continuum. And in the category of permanent housing, another addition to self-sufficiency beckoned.

Self Help Housing: A Preview

In an earlier time, it was common for families to build their own homes: a sod house on the prairie, a log cabin in the woods or even a balloon-frame house at the turn of the century. But the advent of indoor plumbing, electrification and zoning laws mandating housing standards made homebuilding a task for professional builders, and real estate developers provided buyers with tracts of conveniently located, soundly built homes. Good paying jobs and the development of postwar suburbs transformed working-class America into middle-class, home-owning America, and the American dream became focused on owning a split-level with a backyard barbecue pit. But not everyone could attain the dream, and, in the 1960s, socially-motivated—Friends—Quakers—organized the Vinelanders Community Land Trust, a 501(c)3 nonprofit in Kansas City, Missouri, that enabled individuals to build their own homes. The trust organized Self Help builder groups that helped build each other's homes with the assistance of a certified master builder. Their communal labor became the down payment on their houses; this sweat equity and hard, cooperative work made the program a success.

In 1971, the U. S. Department of Agriculture (USDA) adopted the trust's approach and provided two-year operating grants to nonprofit agencies, together with subsidized loans to low-income families participating in the program.

In the spring of 1989, VISTA volunteers Mae Stork and Candy Simon traveled 30 miles north to examine the work of Skagit Self Help Housing, a group making low-income home ownership available through sweat equity. Through an agreement negotiated by Ed with the executive director of Skagit Self Help Housing, Mae and Candy joined Skagit's board to learn how the program worked and returned a year-and-a-half later brimming with expertise and excitement. With Self Help Housing, Housing Hope could provide low-income families an opportunity to step through the door of the American dream and own a home of their own. In December 1990, the Skagit Self Help Housing Board proposed that its grantor, USDA-RD, fund Housing Hope to do a Self Help Housing program in Snohomish County. It also agreed to work with the agency and carry out a Snohomish County feasibility survey and conduct a land search.

From Storming to Forming

Meanwhile, Housing Hope continued to organize itself. When the IRS granted it tax-exempt status as a nonprofit agency, the board set up an account at Frontier Bank with the help of Lyle Ryan, who had also been the banker for Mental Health Services. Personnel benefits were defined. In the interests of frugality during this start-up period, vacation days were limited to six, and board members were each asked to pay the $12.50 cost of attending the United Way training session. On September 1, 1988, the fledging nonprofit was finally able to compensate Ed so he could leave Mental Health Services and work at Housing Hope full time. Ron Wilmot's son, Scott, designed a logo the agency adopted and used on its business cards: a home with the cross superimposed on the house. It was decided that Housing Hope would undergo annual financial audits conducted initially by local firm Wintch, Tobiason & Co.

Mae Stork and her fellow VISTA volunteers tracked their hours as in-kind contributions, which helped to generate data utilized to justify operating grants and leverage new grants. The Everett Job Service Center of the Employment Security Office notified the agency that it was applying for federal Department of Labor funding to serve homeless families. They offered Housing Hope a subcontract to receive funds for a case manager and two employment specialists, to work with homeless individuals. The agency became eligible to receive vouchers and certificates provided for the homeless, and, through funding from the Federal Emergency Management Agency (FEMA) and the Emergency Shelter Assistance Program (ESAP), the Red Cross agreed to make daily reimbursements to the Crossroads shelter of $23 for each homeless family of two to four and $30 for each homeless family of five. At emergency shelters, residents were charged five dollars a night if they could pay; the fee was waived if they could not. On departure, each family was eligible for a loan or a grant to help secure housing.

Housing Hope further defined who among the homeless it would serve: two-parent families, especially large families; mothers or fathers with children; couples if the mother was pregnant; and the mentally ill. The primary focus would be on those at the lower end of the economic spectrum, earning less than 30% of the area's median income, and secondarily on those earning less than 50% of the area's median income. As had been the case with the emergency shelter, the agency's plans for transitional housing were small. This was practical for a small group learning how to do things in the early stages of organizational development, and it also made economic sense.

For several years Housing Hope searched out distressed properties for development. Besides being much cheaper than newer or better preserved structures, they enabled the agency to apply for rehabilitation grants it could use to leverage other grants and loans. This also helped out with public relations: distressed housing usually ended up as low-rent eyesores, magnets for transients, easy targets for break-ins, and a whole slew of threatening activities including arson.

The board also oversaw the development of a policy manual, adopted financial protocols and sent Mae to a workshop to learn how to capture government grants. Through it all, board president Amy Youngstrom's ability to merge the agendas of various groups facilitated the agency's work. "She was a perfect person to have as president," Ed recalled, "because she was widely known and respected in the community". Hers became the lively, energetic and appealing face of Housing Hope on its maiden voyage.

Hope Builders

Now that it had its own building, Housing Hope left the Luther Child Center and opened a new office in studio apartment #6 at Crossroads. The board established a planning committee to develop a one-year plan for 1989 and a five-year plan for the first half of the '90s, and created Hope Builders a new committee which would raise funds, organize volunteer work parties and provide advice on matters of fundraising policy. From the beginning, Hope Builders enjoyed enthusiastic public participation. Newsletters advertised rummage sales, celebrity car washes, supper theaters, bowl-a-thons and a concert

The Original Hope Builders

Barb Stave and Anita Olson at Holiday Bazaar fundraiser

Barb Stave and Anita Olson were two peas in a pod. Both were born in and grew up in north Snohomish County. Both belonged to Our Saviors Lutheran Church in Everett.

Both shared the spiritual perspective that faith without works is dead. They each got involved in the North County Association of Churches in the mid 1980s and were active supporters for the creation of Housing Hope. Barb served on the executive committee of NSCAC that recommended the establishment of Housing Hope. Anita served on the Housing Committee of NSCAC.

In 1989 Barb and Anita agreed to Co-chair Hope Builders. This arm of Housing Hope was initiated by formal action of the Housing Hope board in August 1988. It was the purchase of Crossroads Apartments and the creation of emergency shelter for homeless families that triggered this step. During the next couple of years, under the leadership of these two mission-driven women, the agency rolled out a series of fundraising and friend-making events. These included a rummage sale, a celebrity car wash, a golf tournament, a dinner theater production (the Foreigner at the Elks), a Linda Allen concert, bowl-a-thons, holiday bazaars, a night at the Seattle Mariners, the sale of sweatshirts, and an original play produced and premiered at the Everett Yacht Club. Together these two amazing women put Housing Hope on the philanthropy map in Snohomish County and brought lots of new friends to the agency.

The Truck of Hope

It was a great day in February 1989 when Housing Hope moved its offices and six-month-old staff of four from Crossroads Apartments up on Rucker Hill to Wetmore Avenue in downtown Everett.

The organization was now separated from its emergency shelter facility. The need to maintain the building, move donations, support special events and deliver supplies to residents caused daily challenges.

Board Member Ron Wilmot silently listened and watched during staff discussions and board meetings. Then one day Ron showed up unexpectedly with a carefully selected used Chevy pickup which he indicated would be donated over a three year period. Unfortunately, the next week the truck was driven without oil, resulting in a burned out engine. Ron, the ever-forgiving soul that he was, took the truck and had the engine replaced, and then (probably to avoid any further liability!) decided to donate it immediately. He even helped acquire a magnetic "Housing Hope" sign for each door of the cab. The staff was extremely careful to check the oil regularly from this point forward and the truck served the organization exceedingly well for several years.

Ron served nine years on the board and along with many other marvelous contributions became the "go-to-guy" whenever vehicle purchases, sales and related issues surfaced. He even helped sell a 28-foot boat donated to Housing Hope. Twenty-three years later, in 2012, Ron is involved in helping HopeWorks find a truck for its GroundWorks Landscaping social enterprise.

featuring folk singer Linda Allen, all of which were well attended. An archery contest where archer Paul Peters succeeded in breaking the indoor target world record netted 300 pounds of food and $175 for the Housing Hope food basket drive. Church and school youth groups were organized into work parties to garden and to clean, paint and furnish apartments. When the Lombard Apartments needed painting, Hope Builders put out the word. Thirty-two Windermere Real Estate Realtors spent their Community Service Day donning smocks, picking up brushes and dividing into groups

Housing Hope truck with Ed, Bridget Bischof, Michelle Powers and Aat Bontje

of eight for each exterior wall - and in three hours they had completed a job that would normally have taken all day.

It wasn't long before another office move was warranted. Four staff in a little studio apartment put too many constraints on managing a growing organization. In February 1989, an office in downtown Everett was obtained, complete with reception area, meeting room, offices and storage.

The Maundy Thursday Collection, 1989

On Holy Thursday in 1989 the congregation at St. Cecelia's Roman Catholic Church in Stanwood, a small community 25 miles north of Everett, celebrated a mass commemorating the Last Supper. At the second collection, after his sermon about both rich and poor sharing in God's grace, Father William Treacy collected $453 in an offering from his parishioners for the Crossroads Family Emergency Shelter, which they had adopted as the focus of their mission outreach. Treacy was nationally known as the Roman Catholic panelist on the award-winning KOMO-TV show 'Challenge' where he, Rabbi Raphael Levine and a series of Protestant Ministers discussed and debated serious religious and social issues of the day. He and Levine became close friends, and the installation of a pulpit carved by the rabbi for Treacy's St. Patrick's church on Seattle's Capitol Hill became a nationally televised event celebrating reconciliation between Catholics and Jews, as did Camp Brotherhood, an interfaith retreat center they developed near the city of Mount Vernon in 1975. In the Protestant liturgical calendar, Holy Thursday is called Maundy Thursday, and among the wholly-Protestant founders of Housing Hope, the Maundy Thursday donation became a well-remembered example of ecumenical cooperation. In response to the $453 contribution for Crossroads from Stanwood's St. Cecelia's, Housing Hope followed their example by setting aside the funds to create leverage for a homeless assistance project in Stanwood itself.

Postcard from Father William Treacy

News from Stanwood and Camano Island had highlighted the spread of homelessness there. Were there really homeless people in little Stanwood and on bucolic Camano? John Dean, the managing editor of the Stanwood/Camano News answered the question in an editorial.

A young man walks up to a Stanwood church office, knocks on the door and steps in to ask for help. His mother is outside, he tells the church pastor. They've been living in their car, and they need gas money to make it up to Mount Vernon for a job interview. At another church, a working single mother seeks help, too. She can't find an affordable place to rent and has been living in a tent with her three children. Still other families shuffle back and forth between the area's state and county parks, camping out, stopping off at the food bank, moving on. 'In Stanwood?' Yes. It's happening in Stanwood. [11/29/89]

Camano Island was part of Island County, outside the agency's service area defined in its mission statement, but only a short bridge separated it from Stanwood, the island's market town. In this pastoral setting the image of homeless families living in cars amid lush farms and picturesque villages was a powerful reminder of how serious the problem had become. But critics worried. Did St. Cecelia's adoption of Crossroads mean that Stanwood's and Island County's homeless would become, to paraphrase W. B. Yeats, like some rough beast, slouching toward Everett to be served? And what business was it of Everett's Housing Hope to solve Stanwood's problems?

The Stanwood Action Committee

Treacy facilitated conversations between Housing Hope and the Stanwood ministerium to determine the community's will to address its homeless issue. It was agreed to take action. Local attorney Charles Cole found a home that could be purchased, and he offered free legal assistance toward acquisition. Could local citizens could come together and convert a house into an emergency shelter? The agency suggested Stanwood citizens form the 'Stanwood Housing Hope Action Committee'. In return for Housing Hope's assumption of fiduciary responsibilities, the local committee would ensure grassroots support by helping the agency define the population to be served, create development criteria, explore sites, and facilitate and implement a housing program.

The Stanwood Housing Hope Action Committee chairperson would serve on Housing Hope's Board of Directors to ensure linkage to the agency's broader

Carol Jensen

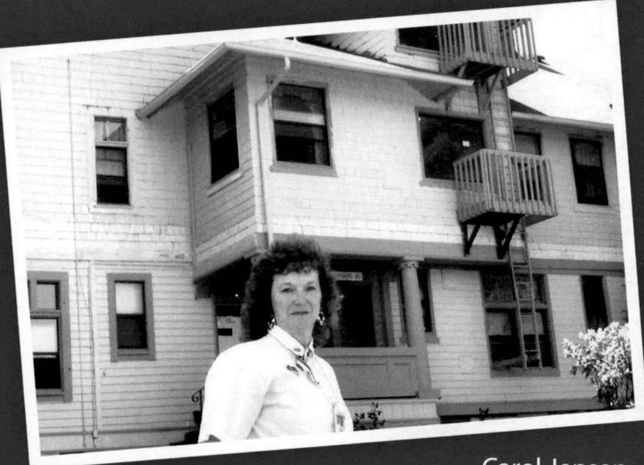

Carol Jensen

In lighthearted moments, Carol Jensen compares herself to Martin Luther: both were rebels and both left the Roman Catholic Church to become Lutherans. During her growing-up years, parents, grandparents and nuns taught her the importance of helping the poor. At a poignant moment during a Stanwood ministerium discussion about Housing Hope in 1989 Carol shared this story:

"...A series of misfortunes sent me and my two daughters to Idaho where I worked as a cocktail waitress. When that job fell through the money ran out. For a week I went without eating in order to feed my daughters until finally, in desperation, I told my old boss that we were at the end of our rope. Moved, he brought over a bag of groceries, paid my rent and helped me get another job."

When Ed asked for volunteers to help start a Housing Hope program in Stanwood, Carol and her friend Jan Leach volunteered to lead the Stanwood Action Committee. Later that year Carol was asked to join the agency's board. Since then she has worked tirelessly, serving as board president and winning awards for her dedication and accomplishments. In Housing Hope's 25th year, Carol still serves on the agency's north branch board and with Stanwood Ambassadors, the outreach group which supports the Housing Hope program in Stanwood.

Charles & Donna Cole

Charles Cole, a Methodist and an attorney, got caught up in the effort to jump start the Housing Hope program in Stanwood.

He helped find a house and donated the legal and escrow services to acquire it. He and Donna remained staunch supporters during their lifetimes and joined the Society of Hope with a bequest in their wills. Their generous gift was added to the Services Endowment Fund where earnings continue to support Stanwood programs for homeless families.

Stanwood House

Charles & Donna Cole

policies. The Action Committee could appoint subcommittees, and, through regular meetings, it would manage the program, public relations and fundraising. The outpouring of popular enthusiasm for this idea is obvious even from the laconic minutes of the Board of Directors meeting which notes that a gathering of 35 people from Stanwood churches, organizations and the city met with representatives from Housing Hope on November 20th to discuss low-income housing needs. This rapidly turned into an organizational meeting which got the ball rolling. Housing Hope's executive committee set up a savings account at Stanwood's SeaFirst Bank to receive local donations, and the bank quickly provided a $26,000 loan to buy the house. To keep the ball rolling, two energetic locals, Carol Jensen from Camano Lutheran Church and Jan Leach from St. Cecelia's, were put in charge of the Stanwood Action Committee. Carol knew some of the homeless families and had been involved in charitable work with Boeing.

The First Stone Soup Dinner

Housing Hope's second anniversary in 1989 generated the plans for what became their annual Stone Soup dinner. The story of Stone Soup is a variant of the parable of the loaves and fishes. In the Stone Soup story, hungry travelers, not trusted by villagers in a small town, put stones in a pot of hot water. Curious villagers come forward to contribute from their meager stock. From one family a potato is contributed, then an onion from another, and carrots from a third, and so on. By sharing what each had, all were able to enjoy a satisfying meal. The Housing Hope Stone Soup dinners began as simple potlucks hosted by Housing Hope in church basements to celebrate successes and thank those whose gifts of time, idealism and service had made the agency possible. More than fifty attended the first, held in Central Lutheran's basement, but as the work grew so did attendance, and so did the dinner's popularity. Eventually the event was moved from church basements into larger, more elegant settings, and became a popular event where corporations, foundations, volunteer groups, churches, other groups and individuals who had distinguished themselves by acts of generosity were given awards that highlighted their contribution to the agency's mission.

Scott foundation supports housing hope

LEONA TOVREA, member of the Scott-Everett Community Affairs Committee, presents Scott's $10,000 contribution to AMY YOUNGSTROM, President of Housing Hope's Board of Directors. Also shown are Ed Peterson, Executive Director, and Todd Morrow, Treasurer.

Local organizations were quick to support Housing Hope. In June 1989, the Northwest Children's Fund granted $10,000 to support the creation of a daycare program, and the Scott Paper Company Employees Fund offered the same. Scott Paper was one of the oldest and best-known businesses in Everett, and Leona Torrea, a member of the Everett Community Affairs Advisory Committee which had recommended Housing Hope to the Fund, underscored its importance: "We feel that this grant will support a new approach to resolving a critical community need—providing emergency shelter to families who need a temporary place to stay. We hope our Scott money will encourage other businesses in the area to get behind Housing Hope and make it a reality."

The City of Everett and Snohomish County together approved more than $25,000 in grants; the County Affordable Housing Trust Fund made an emergency shelter grant of $15,400 and offered a $100,000 loan for the church acquisition and conversion on Harrison Avenue. The Medina Foundation, established in 1947 by Norton Clapp, chairman of the Weyerhaeuser Corporation, granted $18,700. Buoyed by these and others, Housing Hope applied for a grant of $269,638 from the federal Department of Housing and Urban Development (HUD), $350,000 from the Washington State Housing Trust Fund, and $256,771 from the McKinney Fund, all to support new developments. By learning how to weave all this financial spaghetti into a supportive web and leverage it successfully, Housing Hope acquired confidence and credibility in the business community.

In July 1988, after receiving a funding request for Crossroads from Housing Hope, trustees from the Boeing Employees Good Neighbors Fund (BEGNF) visited the Norton Avenue site and suggested the agency withdraw its request for seed money and resubmit a capital request for $45,000 to be part of a capital campaign that would pay down property costs. This was the kernel that later grew into the agency's 1994-1998 Building Hope capital campaign that brought in $1.5 million dollars for new programs. Back in 1985, Central Lutheran's $1,500 contribution had seemed large, but at this stage participants had yet to fully comprehend the scale of the problem.

Chapter 3 Running Uphill: 1990-1994

By the beginning of the new decade, the agency provided emergency shelter at Crossroads and placed families in transitional housing leased from the Red Cross. Permanent affordable housing was available at Crossroads and at the Lombard apartments.

Following its one year plan, it would serve 60 families a year at Crossroads, with a full-time case manager on hand, although Jon Witte recalls that Ed, in his office there, became an additional de facto social worker for its guests. The facilities leased from the Red Cross provided transitional housing for up to two years. CDBG and HUD grant funds enabled the agency's purchase of two houses on Norton Avenue. During conversion and expansion of the houses into eight apartments, while Ed and Todd were standing outside, two men drove up in a red convertible with an elderly woman sitting in the back, her scarf fluttering on the breeze. Bruce Kennedy stepped out to introduce himself and his brother, Duff, and told them how they had grown up in the house. And, hearing of its sale, they wanted to bring their mother, Dorothy, to see it one last time. Ed's explanation of how Housing Hope planned to use it as transitional housing for homeless families impressed them all. Three days later, Housing Hope received an unsolicited check in the mail for $25,000 from the Kennedy Foundation developed by Duff, a successful investment banker. To honor their remarkable gesture Housing Hope named the facility Kennedy Court.

Ed with Dorothy and Bruce Kennedy

Farther up the Snohomish River in the city of Monroe, the St. James Apartments were examined as a possible site for transitional housing outside Everett and the agency approached the Housing Authority of Snohomish County (HASCO) for rehabilitation funding, but this proved premature and the move east was put off for a decade.

The agency's acquisition of a Harrison Avenue property for conversion of an empty church into transitional housing began. With help from the HUD Supportive Housing Program, the agency included an apartment manager unit and eight transitional units to serve homeless and mentally ill mothers at what became known as the Harrison Apartments. In addition to Housing Hope's work in Everett, the Action Committee was busy in Stanwood. With proceeds from a spaghetti dinner and auction fundraiser, rehabilitation of Stanwood House, which would become a family emergency shelter, began. The emergency shelters in Stanwood and at Crossroads, the development of transitional and permanent housing, and housing for the mentally ill were remarkable achievements in Housing Hope's first three years of existence and prompted Ed to note, with no small pride, that "We're on the map now with the County and City."

Harrison Apartments

Tomorrow's Hope children

Tomorrow's Hope

One of the greater problems facing homeless families was finding care for their children when they worked, went to classes or made appointments. Children traumatized by homelessness typically did not do well in normal daycare facilities. Daycare was expensive, and with transportation difficulties, homeless families were hard-pressed even to get their children there. To deal with this, in February of 1990, with a grant from the Northwest Children's Fund, Housing Hope opened Tomorrow's Hope daycare in donated space at the Seventh-day Adventist Church on Federal Avenue. Later this would become the first licensed daycare program for homeless children in Snohomish County. For two half-days a week, parents could leave their children at a safe place to be cared for while they met with doctors, counselors, employers or landlords.

It quickly became apparent that the services the agency hoped to access at other agencies simply did not exist in forms that adequately served homeless families. This sobering reality appears in the earliest organizational charts with their boxes and connecting lines showing the board overseeing the executive director who administered two groups of departments: one group dealing with properties and the other with service programs such as case management and childcare. Another need requiring special attention was to help residents with employment.

When the Private Industry Council (PIC), a local arm of the U. S. Department of Labor, alerted the agency that the Department had issued a Notice of Funding Availability (NOFA) for programs providing job training for the economically disadvantaged and those with disabilities, Housing Hope applied for and received funding for a national demonstration project. Working with the PIC and with Community Trades and Careers, a local non-profit, the project employed two full-time staff members to assess clients' literacy and skills; provide loans and scholarships for job training in construction, retail, community services and business operations; place them in local jobs; and provide follow-up.

The success of Hope Builders in raising public interest in Housing Hope's mission produced enthusiastic offers of help from the community. This effort was enhanced when United Way of Snohomish County, under the leadership of President Tom Unger, made homelessness the focus. Simultaneously, Housing Hope established a new Hospitality Program to provide churches, groups and individuals opportunities for donating services, funds or goods and to help families maintain their apartments. High school volunteers held drives to collect clothing, canned food and funds. Building on the experience of churches who 'adopted' the five shelter apartments at Crossroads, and with assistance from United Way, a fully-fledged adopt-an-apartment program was launched in which churches, businesses, service clubs and schools helped maintain facilities. Tom Unger and his brother-in-law Bob Dent, owners of Tyee Aircraft, had their company adopt apartments at Kennedy Court. Volunteer groups cleaned apartments, landscaped grounds, worked at Tomorrow's Hope and collected money to provide Thanksgiving groceries for adopted families.

At Christmastime, cooks at several schools volunteered to prepare family dinners while Carol Jensen at the BEGNF oversaw Boeing's efforts to fill Christmas stockings for all residents. Volunteering became an eye-opener for many. When Mariner High School senior Lynn Josephson from Mukilteo saw the one-room studio apartment she and her fellow members of the school's DECA program (a local branch of the national Distributive

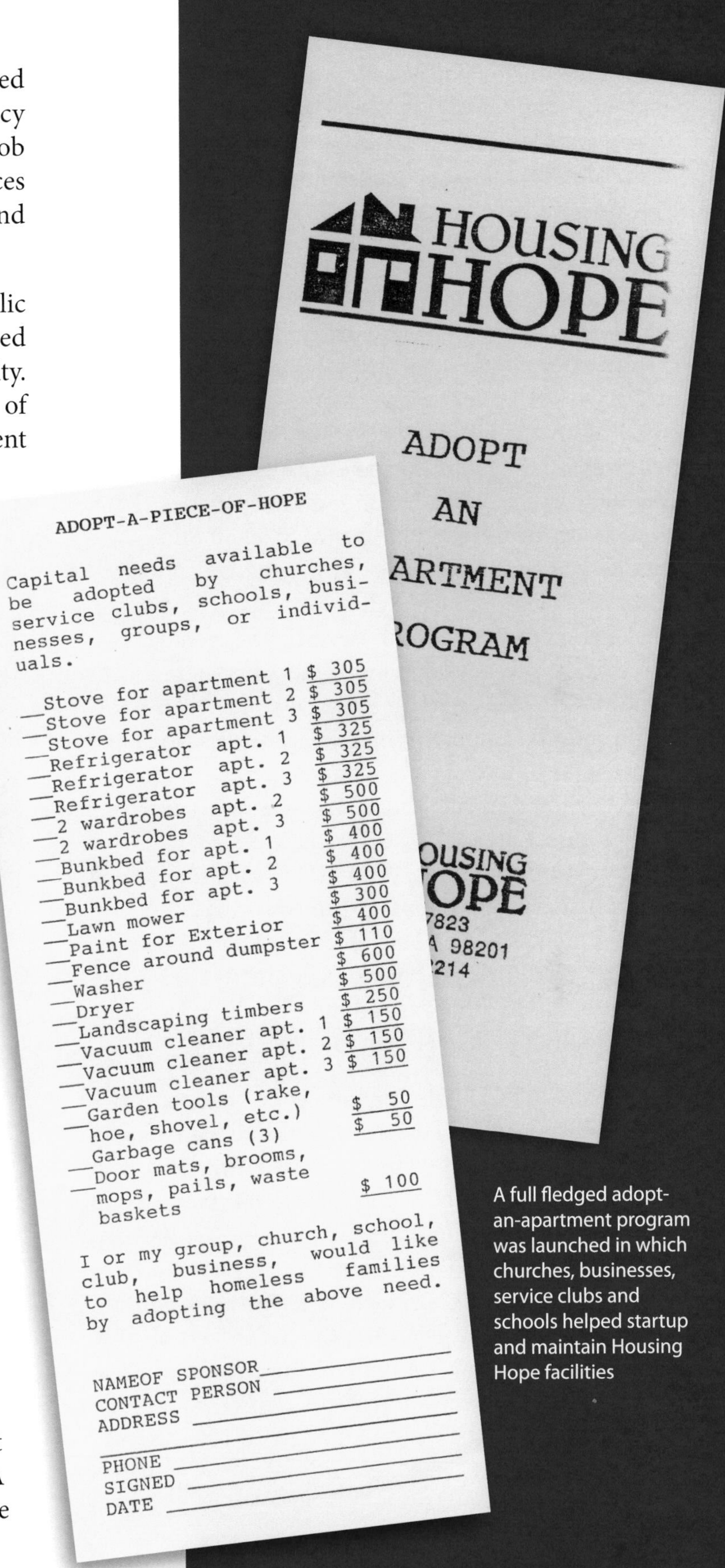

ADOPT-A-PIECE-OF-HOPE

Capital needs available to be adopted by churches, service clubs, schools, businesses, groups, or individuals.

__Stove for apartment 1	$ 305
__Stove for apartment 2	$ 305
__Stove for apartment 3	$ 305
__Refrigerator apt. 1	$ 325
__Refrigerator apt. 2	$ 325
__Refrigerator apt. 3	$ 325
__2 wardrobes apt. 2	$ 500
__2 wardrobes apt. 3	$ 500
__Bunkbed for apt. 1	$ 400
__Bunkbed for apt. 2	$ 400
__Bunkbed for apt. 3	$ 400
__Lawn mower	$ 300
__Paint for Exterior	$ 400
__Fence around dumpster	$ 110
__Washer	$ 600
__Dryer	$ 500
__Landscaping timbers	$ 250
__Vacuum cleaner apt. 1	$ 150
__Vacuum cleaner apt. 2	$ 150
__Vacuum cleaner apt. 3	$ 150
__Garden tools (rake, hoe, shovel, etc.)	$ 50
__Garbage cans (3)	$ 50
__Door mats, brooms, mops, pails, waste baskets	$ 100

I or my group, church, school, club, business, would like to help homeless families by adopting the above need.

NAMEOF SPONSOR ____________
CONTACT PERSON ____________
ADDRESS ____________
____
PHONE ____________
SIGNED ____________
DATE ____________

A full fledged adopt-an-apartment program was launched in which churches, businesses, service clubs and schools helped startup and maintain Housing Hope facilities

Educational Clubs of America) had adopted, with its bathroom and small kitchen, she was shocked. "My bedroom is larger than the whole apartment," she said, amazed. "It makes me realize how much I have and how much I have to give."

Housing Hope turned such heartfelt realizations as Josephson's into informational capital that it used to increase awareness and support. After a local reporter provided training in writing copy for publication, a part-time staffer wrote media releases. There were always great stories: in July the Everett Lions contributed $5000 for furnishings and equipment for Kennedy Court, and a few months later Pioneer Bank made news by offering the agency $2500 if other local lenders would do the same. Nik Halladay convinced Pioneer Bank's CEO, Ralph Schapler, to offer a challenge grant to other banks to help the agency create a revolving pre-development fund, an offer that over time netted Housing Hope $18,000. Frontier Bank, Pioneer Bank, Everett Mutual Bank and Cascade Bank became the local mainstays of financial support for the agency, providing advice and friendship beside loans and grants. Cascade's CEO, Frank McCord, and later Fred Safstrom and Dale Lyski of Everett Mutual, joined the Housing Hope Board. Attuned to these positive developments, Mayor Peter Kinch asked to tour the agency's facilities; afterwards, he invited Housing Hope's board to join him and the city council at a box lunch to discuss the needs of the homeless.

With Crossroads up to code and all five apartments occupied, the agency created a hospitality coordinator position to host special events and help case managers arrange classes to assist families. Group Health established evening clinics for Crossroads and Kennedy Court residents. The lease of a farm house in Edmonds signaled a tentative expansion of transitional housing into the suburban hive of southwest Snohomish County. But Housing Hope made a strategic decision to focus on Everett and the northern part of the county in order to progress and achieve scale there, and the south initiative, as it was called, was postponed.

VISTA Volunteers

In March of 1991, Central Lutheran donated an 11-passenger 1975 Chevrolet van and St. Francis Episcopal Church donated a 9-passenger 1974 LTD station wagon. Besides providing necessary transportation for residents, both ferried children to and from Tomorrow's Hope, and the van was put to work later that summer providing transportation for 15 student volunteers from the East Coast's American Jewish Service Society who spent seven weeks helping with property upkeep.

Van donated by Central Lutheran Church

Working with the federal government, Housing Hope secured its own VISTA volunteer program the following year. Volunteers In Service To America (VISTA) was created by Congress in 1964 as a companion initiative to the Peace Corps. Its purpose was to recruit volunteers for one year of service, for the explicit purpose of developing programs and resources to address poverty in communities around the nation. Housing Hope benefitted immensely from the VISTA program, originally through its connection to Mental Health Services, which loaned its VISTA volunteers to Housing Hope. In 1988, these volunteers helped the organization find the Crossroads property, where the agency's first housing program was initiated. By 1991, Housing Hope was ready to manage its own

The original five Vista Volunteers with staff members Ed and Jeannie Lish

VISTA program and was fortunate to be approved by the National Service Corporation for five VISTA volunteers. Their assignments ranged from helping develop the Tomorrow's Hope childcare program to assisting with startup of Self Help Housing, the sweat equity home ownership project. Just like all departing staff, when volunteers completed their year of service, the board saw to it that each person's contribution was publically acknowledged and a small gift was given in thanks.

More Dismal Statistics

In the debate surrounding whether homelessness in Snohomish County was a temporary phenomenon or bound to get worse, getting worse won hands down. And, as in the 1980s, it did so paradoxically as a consequence of rapid growth. Snohomish County's 337,720 residents in 1980 grew to 465,628 by 1990, an increase of nearly 38%, the largest decadal increase in its history, making it the fastest growing county in the State. In the same period, Everett grew from 54,413 to 69,961, an increase of 28% driven by Boeing's vitality and the U.S. Navy's decision to begin construction of its Everett Home Port. When Willis Tucker became Snohomish County's executive in 1980, Everett's unemployment was 12%; by 1990 it had dropped to 4.3%, a little lower than the state average. A lack of good roads was the only constraint on growth, but the rosy numbers masked troubles facing low-wage earners. Home construction could not keep pace with growth, and housing prices soared. Just among seniors, the numbers on waiting lists for low-income housing told the story: in 1987, there were 350 names; in 1988, 750 names; in 1989, 1250. Good economic news emanating from the Puget Sound region attracted people from across the nation and abroad, but families who spent their savings getting here discovered it cost between $1200 and $1800 to pay the first and last month's rent plus a damage deposit. And the time lag between the down payment and the arrival of the first pay check could be very long. By 1990, 22,000 county families were earning less than 30% of the state median wage; housing costs took up 60 to 70% of that, and 31,000 families could not afford housing at all.

Ed Petersen told a Herald Reporter, "You can hear them on the phone when you say you have no room. You hear them crying; you can hear children in the background screaming." Two new groups of homeless emerged: newcomers who could not afford steep rents and natives who could no longer pay them.

Writing about Housing Hope in the Herald, Thomas MacIntyre, executive director of Catholic Community Services in Everett, underscored the stark reality facing the county. Housing Hope had been awarded $269,000 in McKinney grants. He indicated that there had been 399 applicant projects from around the country; 131 were funded—11 in King County, but only one in Pierce County and one in Snohomish County. McKinney funds required local matching funds, and the distribution of grants reflected local government's commitment to low-income housing or, by inference, its lack. Mae Stork wrote an equally blunt letter to the Herald's editor.

...Do we develop more and more shelters to provide temporary beds? Do we develop more and more programs to help the growing numbers of homeless people who have to deal with the emotional problems as a result of their plight? Do we try to find additional dollars to provide more special education programs for kids who are having learning problems because of insecurity of not knowing where home will be tomorrow? We will probably need more law enforcement people and more courts to deal with the domestic violence scene and more recovery programs for alcohol and substance abusers. Is that the way we want to spend our limited resources? Or are we ready to get moving to provide resources for the solution: more low cost housing?"

– Mae Stork

Self Help Housing, A Reality

In May of 1991, the agency started planning its own Self Help Housing Program with a $10,000 pre-development grant from the federal Farmers Home Administration (FmHA). Eight lots were purchased at 9th and Orchard Street in Gold Bar, a little foothill town on Highway 2 leading to Stevens Pass. With $750 a set of house plans was purchased from Whatcom Self Help Housing for 1000-square-foot, one-story ramblers with one to two bathrooms and three or more bedrooms. Staff from Whatcom Self Help assisted Housing Hope properties staff to interview prospective low-income family participants. Once accepted into the program they could receive a subsidized loan from the FmHA. When their homes were completed families received title to the house for far less than it would cost on the market.

By 1990, the price of a house in Snohomish County averaged $147,000, but even if the house price were halved, that is, made cheaper, low-income people could hardly afford it. The ability to manage such debt required a family's breadwinner have a full-time job and a good credit rating. Consistent with its mission, the agency targeted 40% of the participants to be households earning less than 50% of the area's median income. All units had to meet the minimum requirements of the state's Uniform Housing Code, but projects also needed to be financially feasible based on a family's ability to pay their mortgage, which is to say that Housing Hope needed to plan carefully in order to provide permanent housing at prices the low-income household could afford.

Eight heads of families agreed to become the first 'family builders' and spend 30 hours a week for 8-12 months working as a team with other families to build each other's homes, hewing to a bracing schedule not unlike that in an old-fashioned barn-raising. The teams were named and numbered; each was provided a construction supervisor hired to train and supervise them while electrical work, plumbing and sheet rocking was sub-contracted. Sweat produced the equity. Families qualified for loans through FmHA but made no down payment or monthly payments until their home was completed and occupied. As Group 1 began work at Gold Bar the agency submitted requests for $300,000 to purchase sixteen lots at the rural Lake Alyson subdivision in Arlington and would purchase 16 more near Granite Falls at the Blue Spruce subdivision.

The Herald, Saturday, July 10, 1993

Nancy Bransom and her 4-year-old daughter Sarah test the driveway in front of their new home in Gold Bar.

The Herald/JIM LEO

Home sweat home

Cooperative housing venture about finished

By ROBIN STANTON
Herald Writer

GOLD BAR — It's homecoming time for eight families this weekend.

After 10 months of swinging hammers, digging dirt and wielding paint brushes they're ready to move into the homes they built with the help of Housing Hope in this tiny mountain town.

"It's been a real community effort," said Nancy Bransom, sitting in the empty living room of her white-trimmed pink house. She and the other members of Project Premier were gearing up for the ribbon-cutting ceremony Friday that marked the end of their labors.

The eight families in the Gold Bar project were granted zero-down, low-interest federal loans covering the cost of the land and building materials. In exchange, each family provided at least 30 hours of labor a week, or about 65 percent of the labor needed for the project.

Working under the guidance of construction superintendent Tim Howland, everyone worked together to build each house. They subcontracted the electrical work, the plumbing and the Sheetrocking, but performed the rest of the labor themselves. Although they could get help from friends and family members to meet the 30-hour requirement, homeowners had to work at least 15 hours themselves.

Each family will pay about $75,000, or about $15,000 less than the market rate, for their new homes. All the homes are about 1,000 square feet, have three bedrooms and a one-car garage.

This is the first project of its kind in Snohomish County, Sheryl Hull of Housing Hope said. She has another group of eight families who will start building in Granite Falls in about two weeks, and a third group who will start in the fall. Where the projects are built depends on where Housing Hope can find affordable land, she said.

As well as working together on the building project, the Gold Bar families are cooperating in other ways. They take turns caring for each other's children while their parents work on the houses, and many of the 17 children are fast friends. But they are all eager to get moved in and resume some sort of normal life.

"We all kind of need our own space now," Bransom said.

One of the conditions of the project is that none of the families can move in until all the houses are completed. People were eager to finish up in time for Friday's open house, Chris Shaner said.

"Some people were here till 1 a.m. last night," he said. Some planned to begin moving in right after the open house was over, others wanted to take the weekend off.

"I've essentially been working three jobs through this whole time," Shaner said. He works 10-hour days milling lumber at a cabinet shop four days a week, delivers pizza in the evenings, and put in his 30 hours a week on the building project.

He and his wife Laurie had one daughter when they began this project. Now they also have 2-month-old twin sons. Laurie spent much of the winter and spring on full bed rest, and in and out of hospitals. They're looking forward to spending time together as a family again.

Bransom, single mother of a 9-year-old boy and 4-year-old girl, said finding time for her family was the hardest part of the project. She works full time at the Snohomish Health District.

Her daughter, Sarah, got an ear infection in mid-February that required hospitalization and surgery. While recovering, Sarah wanted her mom. "They'd call me from the child care and say she couldn't walk, her ear hurt so much," Bransom said. "I thought, this isn't worth it. I'll live in an apartment the rest of my life, but I want to be with my daughter."

But she got through it, week by week, and the payoff was worth it, she said.

"She lived, I lived, and here we are," she said.

Sarah herself was bright and bubbly Friday, eager for the party to start and happy to see all her friends.

First Self Help Housing site makes headlines

The Arlington Action Committee, 1991

Stanwood's Mayor, Bob Larson, told Ed that he really liked what Housing Hope was doing in his town, and that he would help it replicate its work in other communities. When Pastor Gordon Pease's Peace Lutheran Church in the town of Silvana collected $600 during its 1990 Fat Tuesday Mardi Gras celebration and donated it to Housing Hope, the agency dedicated the amount for a yet-to-be-determined project in Arlington. The goal was to replicate the success of leveraging the Maundy Thursday donation from St. Cecelia's parish in Stanwood.

Peace Lutheran's contribution had called Housing Hope's attention to the homeless problem in Arlington. The city's planning committee and its chamber of commerce sought to deal with this issue. Several members of the Stanwood Action Committee were invited to tell their story to community leaders, and an Arlington Action Committee was organized with Pastor Pease as a leading member. By November, the Arlington Action Committee had raised another $3000. This, added to the $600, was used to leverage funds to purchase Housing Hope's fourth property, an abandoned house that looked totally woebegone in its overgrown yard; this house would be converted into three units of transitional housing. It happened that Bob Larson was also on the County Block Grant Committee, and the Snohomish County Housing Trust Fund advised the agency that $57,000 was awarded to them for a rehabilitation project. Using the donations and strong local support as leverage, Housing Hope also submitted a proposal to the State of Washington Housing Trust Fund.

The role that faith communities played in Housing Hope's development cannot be overemphasized. In a very real way, Stanwood's and Arlington's offerings recall another moment in Northwest history when American Protestant missionaries believed they heard what they called the 'Macedonian cry' emanating from

Native American groups, after the cry Paul heard in his vision recorded in Acts 16:9, 'Come over to Macedonia to help us'. Housing Hope was organized under the aegis of the NSCAC and the dynamism it drew from the religious enthusiasm of several congregations was matched by the enthusiasm of congregations in outlying communities. They all shared the same commitment and were fired by the same zeal which found poignant realization in picnics arranged so that local residents could sit down to meet and eat with those they served. This had not been done before, and it recalled the fellowship of the table described in Luke's Acts of the Apostles where gentile and Jew came together to share a commemorative meal as children of God. Reflecting on communities' zeal for good works, Ed told a Herald Reporter, "I'm sure a lot of it comes from the Gospels and the dedication to be of service," but he and the agency determined not to distract people from the issue of homelessness by proselytizing for any particular religious viewpoint. They did not need to.

But the road traveled in Arlington was not as serendipitous as the description thus far might make it appear. After the abandoned house was torn down, the new facility had to be built on the same footprint, and one wall from the old structure retained in order to be eligible for rehabilitation funding. But when the state Housing Trust Fund denied Housing Hope's funding request, one of the three planned transitional units was converted into permanent housing. Section 8 of the federal Rental Assistance Program provided rent subsidies to low-income individuals who could lease permanent housing thus providing market-rate income to the property. What the State denied with one hand, creative financing could make up for with the other.

But, there was no getting around the loss of a staff position when the Private Industry Council defunded part of Housing Hope's adult job training program. The Council required that at least 25 individuals be placed in stable employment per year, but the agency had only placed 16. Given that it was dealing with

Arlington Triplex before and after

the homeless, who nobody else wanted to work with and who had to overcome all sorts of barriers, this was, in fact, a huge accomplishment, but because it did not meet the minimum requirement, funding was reduced. Additional problems came when three of the Lombard apartments had to be closed temporarily due to problems with plumbing and with the foundation. When the agency's computer system crashed in the spring of '91, completion of the previous year's financial report was delayed pending the hiring of a troubleshooter and the theft that fall of the computer holding its fiscal records made matters even worse.

The Wrath Of The Electorate

Yet these problems paled in comparison to what was coming. The need for housing was desperate: 54,000 people were expected to move in as work on the 777 jetliner got underway, and what was already the world's largest building at Boeing's Everett plant nearly doubled in size to accommodate production. In addition, more than 18,000 were expected to arrive with the construction of the Navy's homeport. So in September, the county placed a 10-year, $54 million low-income housing levy on the ballot. Boeing spent $25,000 to support the levy and Frank McCord, of Everett's Cascade Bank, led a citizen's committee that argued passionately for low-income housing. The present-day reader may wonder at the novelty of a bank president actually caring about low-income housing, but this was when most banks were still locally owned and bankers cared about customers' welfare as well as the bottom line. And McCord was committed: he noted that 21,000 families in the county —60,000 individuals, many of them children—were homeless or at risk. In 1987, 2,600 requests for shelter had been denied; in 1990, 8,600 people were turned away and of these, 90% were families with children. This levy would provide 1,162 low-income housing units, a small part of what was necessary, but it was a start. Homeowners would pay only $34 per $100,000 valuation, and the amount would be reduced yearly as property values increased. County Executive Bob Drewel and United Way CEO Jack Healy teamed up with McCord to lead the levy campaign.

Even so, the levy, which required 50% voter approval to pass, was soundly defeated by more than 60% of the electorate. Some surmised that fear of new taxes (Edmonds School District also had a levy request on the ballot) led to defeat, but other voters said they didn't think the county had that many homeless. "The reason you don't see them," countered Bob Dickey, chaplain at Union Gospel Mission, "is because they don't want you to see them. The last thing they've got is pride". Seattle Times reporter Jolayne Houtz wrote, "They sleep in their cars in strip-mall parking lots near Alderwood Mall and rest areas around Everett. They break into abandoned homes or crowd in with friends and families. They use up their savings to stay in a motel, then move to a campground."

In 1991, Housing Hope provided 26,843 bed-nights of shelter and transitional housing and day care to 144 children of homeless and low-income parents, a small percentage of those in need. By then Housing Hope was recognized as a lead agency serving homeless families in the county.

Fortunately, Housing Hope did not have to suffer the mood of the electorate. In a short essay that appeared nationally, Oregon Methodist pastor Frank Shields argued that the public's sour mood derived from a perfectionist mentality based on the notion that any program to help the homeless had to be huge and therefore hugely expensive. Many envisioned an enormous bureaucratic system ensnaring vast numbers of the poor, a dehumanizing image that, combined with the constant rain of grim statistics and images, paralyzed good intentions. The trick, he went on to write, was to understand that "You can't handle the whole problem, [but] you take your bite-sized chunk and I'll take mine." Pastor Shields' approach was to provide shelter in church buildings, but there had always been a deep, latent desire in the community to do more. Shirley Morrow recalled a meeting at United Methodist when solutions to the problem of hunger were debated and debated and debated until someone finally pleaded, "Can't we just DO something?" Ed's community organizing skills were helpful, because citizens provided the energy, and were indeed eager to do still more.

When the Stanwood shelter needed a new roof, Rich Menzel, a local contractor, volunteered to tear off the old one and put on a new one gratis. Carol Jensen and the Stanwood Action Committee swung into action and organized a fundraiser, getting Hamilton Lumber, Cascade Lumber and ABR Roofing to donate the materials that were needed. The problem of homelessness in the Stanwood area proved so pressing that the three-bedroom Stanwood House shelter had to turn away nine out of every ten applicants when it opened, but an undaunted and expanded Stanwood/Camano Action Committee immediately began a search to find property for a new and larger housing facility and started working to raise the estimated $1.1 million needed toward construction. And Rich Menzel joined Housing Hope's board and has never stopped volunteering to fix Housing Hope's roofs as needed.

Growing Pains

In 1989 when Housing Hope's office could no longer fit in apartment #6, it had rented Pete Kinch's large apartment above his photo studio in downtown Everett on Wetmore Avenue. This proved insufficient all too quickly, and in '91 the agency found room to expand through a friend of the agency, Ray Sievers, CEO of H. O. Seiffert Company, and moved into the old KRKO radio studio at 3004 Fulton. Fortunately

Rich The Roofer

Rich Menzel

When you're a housing agency it's nice to have a roofer around. Rich Menzel likes roofing. In 1992 Rich joined the Housing Hope team as a Board Member. From that day forward, Rich monitored every roof that came Housing Hope's way.

Whenever asked, he helped diagnose roof problems and propose solutions. When performance issues arose with roofing contractors, he would assess the job, define quality standards and would urge Housing Hope to not accept the work unless it was done to standard. Rich helped family builders in the first sweat equity group with their roofing. Not only that, but he also repaired many of Housing Hope's roofs himself, and led volunteer work parties to replace the roofs on Stanwood House and the Harrison Apartments.

Menzel Roofing is Rich's company. He works by himself because he likes it that way. There are few who can live up to his extremely high quality standards and unbelievable work ethic. A former Navy Seal, Rich has a body of steel to go with his heart of gold. Rich Menzel was elected to the Housing Hope Board of Directors in 1992 and served nine years, becoming a Board Member Emeritus in 2001. He has also served twenty years on the Housing Hope Properties Board, filling a spot representing his low-income neighborhood.

the youth from the American Jewish Service Society were available to help clean and renovate the empty building. Its cubicles had glass upper walls that enabled disk jockeys to observe the antics of their fellows, but the views were soon blocked by stacks of housing supplies, and meetings were often held between bales of Huggies, bags of clothing and pallets of toilet paper.

Tomorrow's Hope had also outgrown its very temporary home at the Adventist Church and moved that same year to donated space at Calvary Lutheran Church, just around the corner from the new office, on 26th Avenue. Hours were doubled to 20 per week for 26 children and the program was enhanced with a new health clinic coordinated by Carol Petersen and Lori Prins of Community Health Center, to offer immunizations, checkups and referrals. But it would have to move again in 1993, this time to the lower level of Bill Brust's dental office on 41st Street, where the number of children it could serve increased to 30, finally in an all day program. Unfortunately, this took it farther away from the office, which hindered communication.

Eventually this little daycare was able to become the lead childcare provider in the county for vulnerable children, and would provide its services to the children of homeless families served by other providers such as VOA, YWCA, Everett Gospel Mission, Domestic Violence Services and the Interfaith Association of Snohomish County.

Housing Hope Properties, 1992

The disconnect between electoral angst and communal generosity did not reduce the necessity of Housing Hope's scrambling to find funds for its growing programs. Several years were required to move a project from the planning stage to a ribbon cutting, and the agency typically managed several projects at once. But as strategic plans became more involved, so did funding, and the agency was always on the lookout for new creative strategies. In 1990,

Kids' Clinic

Children get sick. Parents don't know what to do. There's no primary care provider. The money runs out. Homeless families taught us many things in our early years. Learning about the fragility of health and the dearth of available resources helped open our eyes.

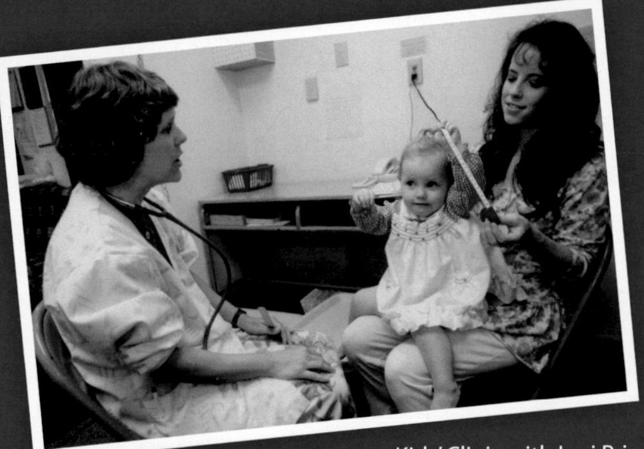

Kids' Clinic with Lori Prins

In 1992, Housing Hope had embarked on an expansion of its neophyte childcare program, Tomorrow's Hope. Ed discussed the healthcare challenge with his wife Carol and she became an advocate for a solution through Community Health Center of Snohomish County (CHC), where she worked as a medical social worker. CHC, a federally-certified low-income health clinic, enthusiastically agreed to partner in addressing this need and extended this service to homeless teens at Cocoon House as well.

For the next eight years, Carol and Nurse Practitioner Lori Prins collaborated on staffing the once-a-week Kids' Clinic onsite at Tomorrow's Hope. This team provided well-child checks, immunizations, consultations to staff, education for parents, and they facilitated access to healthcare services and medical coverage for children.

Kids' Clinic has moved, along with Tomorrow's Hope, four times and is in its nineteenth year of operations. New providers have stepped into Carol and Lori's shoes, including Nurse Practitioner Vicky Fox, who has staffed the clinic since 2006. These Kids' Clinic champions, along with CHC, are appreciated for their impact and admired for their passion for healthy kids.

Congress passed the Cranston-Gonzales National Affordable Housing Act to create a nationwide capacity-building initiative. This funded organizations dedicated to helping the country address its affordable housing challenge. It did this by funding community housing development organizations (CHDO), that required at least one third of their membership be low-income or represent a low-income community. Housing Hope could have become a CHDO but did not want to surrender one third of its multi-tasking board to satisfy the requirement, so in 1992 it created a membership agency, Housing Hope Properties (HHP), that had only one member—Housing Hope. HHP was organized as a separate 501(c)3 non-profit. Housing Hope's board retained the authority to appoint HHP's board of directors and president. As a CHDO, HHP met the government's organizational requirements and applied for and received HUD grants that Housing Hope could not.

HHP became the housing development arm of Housing Hope, planning development activities, and HHP's board worked closely with its parent agency, in a transparent, overlapping way by discussing all resolutions or plans with Housing Hope's board to minimize unpleasant surprises. It is important to note that while Housing Hope and its subsidiary agencies have encountered many challenges along the way as a result of these complex arrangements, it has not suffered scandal—in spite of the many millions of dollars that have passed through multiple hands, there has been not one incident of fraud. Housing Hope maintained this high standard by closely examining the people it recruited and following carefully crafted business practices, and contracting annually for consolidated financial and compliance audits of its affiliated agencies. To ensure public confidence in its mission and its reputation as a good steward, Housing Hope dotted every 'i,' crossed every 't' and counted every penny.

The HOF

As one of its first acts, Housing Hope Properties created the Housing Opportunity Fund (HOF), a revolving fund that received donations and was constantly replenished to provide feasibility study funds and earnest money to purchase property for multi-family projects when opportunities arose. The $18,000 that Pioneer Bank's challenge grant produced was the seed money. Later the HOF was increased through grants received and was included in capital campaigns to grow the balance to $300,000. It also became the recipient of Equity Equivalent Investments (known as EQ2 loans, which are preferential and potentially forgivable loans) from Wells Fargo Bank and U.S. Bank. Combined, these loans totaled $600,000, increasing the HOF to over $900,000.

There were good reasons for banks to make these EQ2 loans. In 1977 Congress passed the Community Reinvestment Act (CRA), which addressed the discriminatory lending practice known as 'redlining,' whereby commercial entities withheld services in communities deemed to be poor financial risks. Actual red lines on maps circumscribed such poor communities that typically were occupied by African-Americans as well as other minorities. Among its provisions, the law required that banks offer credit to borrowers in all communities where they were chartered, including moderate- and low-income neighborhoods, and it instructed federal financial supervising agencies to take bank compliance with this law into consideration when approving applications for new branches, mergers or acquisitions. Because Snohomish County had a relatively thin infrastructure of social agencies dedicated to helping the low-income population, the appearance of Housing Hope as a reliable agency was a boon and because of this, banks actively courted Housing Hope and offered generous loans and grants that built up the HOF and assisted its development projects.

When Pioneer Bank was acquired by Washington Mutual (WAMU) in 1993, its strong relationship with Housing Hope continued under the guidance of Tim

Otani, Director of the Washington Mutual Foundation. He took an interest in Housing Hope and Snohomish County by serving on committees that met from 1993 to 1995 to organize three Building Solutions housing conferences. WAMU had two priorities for charitable giving: promoting public education and providing for affordable housing, and in the latter category Tim asked Housing Hope to review its plans and needs annually and tell him, over a lunch he provided, what financial support it desired from the foundation. Tim prioritized these needs, and coached Housing Hope on how to apply for what became $20,000, $30,000 and $50,000 annual grant amounts. WAMU also provided a $10,000 yearly Sponsorship for Stone Soup dinners and became a presenting sponsor for the Windermere Golf Tournament. Housing Hope had a good friend in WAMU, with Tim's support, until WAMU's dramatic demise in 2008.

Good News From Gold Bar

In June of 1992, the first eight families were selected for Self Help Housing, and that fall work at Gold Bar was underway. Under the supervision of Program Manager Greg Bradley and Construction Supervisor Tim Howland, a former architect and contractor who ran his own company for 22 years, Group 1 raised one house after the other. "Today we're working on my house, putting the walls up" said Nancy Branson, 27, a single mother of two. "For me there'd be no way of owning a home, especially being a single parent. No way. When this came through I just got so lucky. This is the only way I'm going to get a home."

---

23 year-old Chris Shaner and his wife and daughter had been living with relatives, but now he could look forward to a different future. "I love dogs; now I can get one. Here we'll have the perfect back yard for it... I'll have a nice garden and a whole big front yard."

Women home builders

The group was learning both building construction and teamwork skills. Many had never worn a carpenter's apron or handled a power saw, but they learned how and worked together under the tutelage of Housing Hope's construction supervisor. Others had already organized a cooperative daycare for the group's 14 children. And watching the group work in rain or shine, the neighbors responded. "The community has been great" said Branson; "The first week we were out here, people we don't even know were dropping by tools. They'd say 'Just drop them off on your way home. Come meet us if you need help.'" Another builder, Cary Rupert summed up the prevailing spirit. "Over there at the back wall is our bedroom; there's the third bedroom. That corner there will be the kitchen with a dining area in the front, and here's the living room. Everybody's really motivated to get it done. Everybody wants their house."

In the 1600s William Bradford, the governor of Plymouth Colony, recorded in his account Of Plimouth Plantation that each Mayflower family was given a small plot and seeds in a desperate effort to increase the food supply. They had spent three miserable years working for the colony and starving, but the experiment, '...made all hands very industrious. ...the women now went willingly into the field and took their little ones with them..." This was something new. The idea that individual effort nurtured by a supportive community could produce benefit for all— in this case a food surplus—began as an American experiment, and on a rainy November

Kennedy Court 1991

Century House work party

Saturday in Goldbar, a new group of pilgrims repeated the gamble of their predecessors. Not all or even most of those who graduated from transitional housing would enter Housing Hope's Self Help Housing Program, but for those who did and for those other low income people, being able to own their own home was powerful insurance against ending up on the street. A year later, in August, several dozen more pilgrims grouped in sixteen low-income families—Groups 2 and 3—began work on their homes in the Lake Alyson subdivision near Granite Falls.

More Transitional Housing

Three duplexes and a house at Kennedy Court opened in January of 1991 as the first transitional housing facility in Snohomish County, providing seven units for homeless families. In July, 1992, the Harrison Apartments opened with nine units, and in March of 1993, 50 invitees applauded the ribbon cutting at the new Arlington Triplex. Its first resident manager, Mike Winslow, had driven a truck until an injury cost him his job and his family became homeless. Graduating from Housing Hope's transitional housing program in Stanwood, he enrolled in Housing Hope's Employment and Training programs and attended community college, overcoming a learning disability. Now fully employed, he continues parenting his children and has rebuilt his life in his own home.

Century House, 1993

First Presbyterian planned to celebrate its 1993 centennial by installing a 2060-pipe Balcom and Vaughan organ, but in the drive to raise the necessary $300,000, many wondered if money should also be raised for the church's social ministry. The congregation raised an additional $50,000 and presented it to Housing Hope as a challenge grant to address the needs of homeless pregnant women. Most of these were young; many had been kicked out of their homes or were fleeing dangerous situations. Those more fortunate moved in with kin, others with friends—termed 'couch surfing'—while others lived on the streets. It was largely a hidden problem until the fall of 1991, when their growing numbers became news as 12 homeless and pregnant young women sought shelter at Everett Gospel Mission's Women's Refuge Center.

In February of 1992, the agency put down earnest money for a house on Everett Avenue once owned by a prominent Everett physician, Dr. Nathan Thompson, whose children had been born and raised there. The facility would be named Century House in honor of First Presbyterian's centennial and would house four homeless pregnant women ages 18 to 24 with no other child, each mom and baby having their own private bedroom and all sharing two bathrooms, two kitchens, a living room, laundry facilities and a yard. The program was supported by Deaconess Children's Services and the state Department of Social and Health Services. A social worker from Olympic Mental Health, Sharon Mation, provided the women training in well-baby care, parenting, household management and helped them finish school and find employment. Gloria Keliiaa served as Housing Hope's first case manager, and Tomorrow's Hope provided day care.

Housing Hope Is Made Homeless

That summer Housing Hope learned that it was about to become homeless. Eagle Hardware, needing 540 parking spaces for its hardware box store, had purchased property including the KRKO building on Fulton Street, and Housing Hopes offices were scheduled to be torn down. Fortunately and rather amazingly, Aat had managed to locate an empty award-winning office building owned by the Jeld-Wen door company on the Everett waterfront. Resembling a fortress from the outside, it had been designed by local architect Robert Champion for the E.A. Nord Company, one of the world's largest wooden door manufacturers. In 1983, Nord was on the eve of a strike called by local 1054 of the United Brotherhood of Carpenters and Joiners of America. Recalling the bloody 1919 Industrial Workers of the World strike against David Clough's Pacific Lumber Mill, when an owner facing diminishing profit margins determined to break a union of desperate workers, the Nord Door strike, while bloodless, was hardly less bitter. Rather than breaking the union, however, Nord Door "broke itself" and filed for bankruptcy in 1986. It was bought out by Jeld-Wen, which decided that the building - with its glass interior, water fountain and flying bridge office where an ersatz Darth Vader could observe his laboring minions - carried too much negative baggage, closed this office space down, moved its management into the plant with its workers, and put the fortress out for rent.

Tomorrow's Hope children at Jeld-Wen

In return for refurbishing an essentially abandoned building, Housing Hope received four months of free rent. Part of the space could be adapted for Tomorrow's Hope, which could once again be brought back in closer proximity. It wasn't a complete plus: the number of childcare slots at Jeld-Wen had to be reduced to 26 and the building's isolated location on Everett's somnolent northern waterfront presented a problem, especially for parents transporting their children to and from the less-than-peaceful site, where railroad cars slammed loudly into one another on the siding across the road. Although it was aesthetically striking, the agency longed for a permanent home of its own.

Todd Becomes President

In July, Amy Youngstrom stepped down from five years as 'temporary' president of the board after its members finally got around to electing a replacement, Todd Morrow. Amy's husband, George, was relieved; he always thought Amy worked too hard, and she assured him she would take it easy from then on. Her calendar appeared blissfully clear of appointments, but when he remarked that she still seemed to attend a lot of meetings, she confessed to have simply stopped writing them down because she didn't want him to worry.

One of Todd's first responsibilities was a stakeout with Ed. Not long after Kennedy Court's opening, neighbors complained that it had become a site for drug dealing. The problems some homeless brought with them spilled out into the community, which took notice. The agency moved to solve the problem, but when called, the police department complained of being overworked, and told the agency to contact the county's drug task force. The drug task force was also overworked, and told the agency that documentation was needed before they would act. So, president Todd Morrow and executive director Ed Petersen drove silently to Kennedy Court at a late hour and parked across the street. Among the tools they brought for surveillance, Todd included popcorn. Hours passed; binoculars revealed furtive figures exchanging plastic bags. By 2:00 AM, with license plate numbers duly recorded, Ed and Todd rolled away in a muffled crunch of gravel. The county got documentation and the dealers were apprehended. Happily, in its over twenty years of operation, only few such incidents have occurred at Kennedy Court.

Katherine Cook: From Homeless Family To Board Member

Katherine Cook

Katherine and Homer Cook, along with their four children were homeless in 1992. First sheltered at Crossroads, they entered the transitional housing program at Kennedy Court. It was just what the family needed to stay together and thrive.

Upon departing from Kennedy Court, Katherine was recruited to the board of directors, where she served for nine years and assisted with the Housing Hope Speakers Bureau, telling her story far and wide. She continues to serve on the Housing Hope Properties board of directors.

Chapter 4 Building Hope And A Village: 1994-2000

Storming

The science of creating community organizations has its own lexicon, often capturing memorable concepts that help to describe processes. Storming is figuring out how to make things happen. From the beginning Housing Hope stormed in a seat-of-the-pants sort of way, exploring and dealing with problems as they arose.

Storming is creative, chaotic, free flowing and fun because energy and passion drives discussion and the mission. Forming happens when a group comes together, defines its purpose, creates a structure and sets its ground rules. By the early '90s, the agency had done much of the work that gave it its resilient form and helped it grow. In order to operate within its means the agency had built small housing developments, but as capacity grew and its track record gave it confidence, it began planning and developing larger projects to make gains on the large and growing need. Scaled up projects also required scaled up fundraising, and Housing Hope entered a phase where storming again took on new dimensions, promising new risk but also new opportunities. And instead of a building or a house, the agency began to think of creating a village.

The Mignacco Mansion, 1994

Two housing village projects were planned. For this, Housing Hope needed to organize a capital campaign to raise $1.5 million, and investigate new sources of funding. The target of the capital campaign, christened 'Building Hope,' was the construction of facilities to meet the expanding needs of Tomorrow's Hope, provide 19 apartments for homeless and low-income families, and create a permanent space for the agency's offices. Housing Hope could finally settle down. "We've had to move four times," Ed observed, "I thought, let's finally get a home of our own." To get the campaign going, ten board members collectively pledged $25,000 dollars. The challenge was great, however, a sense of success enabled the agency to think in terms not limited to shelters or services, but encompassing a community where people could restore their essential humanity. Ed summed up the challenge in a question: "Can we create a village where people take care of each other?" And this was many years before Hillary Clinton wrote her best-seller, "It Takes A Village: And Other Lessons Children Teach Us".

And to find a site for such a village, Aat had been a busy man. As one who liked working with his hands, he joined contractors in gutting the Lombard apartments, and rebuilding Kennedy Court and the Harrison Apartments. He knew what he was looking for, and he found what he believed was the perfect spot: the old Mignacco mansion on Evergreen Way.

Built in 1927, the two story house with a hipped roof originally featured a semi-circular cobblestone driveway and lovely fountain in the front yard. An extensive orchard and a caretaker's house were located in back. In 1937 Michael Mignacco, a popular Everett restaurateur, bought the property after its owner's divorce, and it became a social hub for the city. In those days, Evergreen Way was the Pacific Highway (Highway 99), with restaurants, night clubs, card parlors, bars and more strung out between Portland and Bellingham. Fred Safstrom, the president of Cascade Bank, remembered delivering newspapers at the elegant house as a kid and stealing apples from the orchard, and local politicos including Senator Henry

Jackson were common visitors to the elegant home. But after the Mignacco family moved out and converted the house to a rental in the 1970s, it fell on hard times and eventually became a haven for junkies who discarded their needles into the crowding vegetation. When Aat brought Ed to see it he was flabbergasted but not speechless. "There were vines coming out of broken windows! We found an abandoned car there one day! What had once been a wonderful jewel... had become a gaping hole!" Did Aat have holes in his head? But he pointed out the value of nearly two acres next to a purling, albeit polluted, stream and the structural integrity of the house. And because it had a history, they could garner community support and tax credits for its preservation. Ed conceded, and after a long and protracted negotiation with the Mignacco heirs, the agency put down earnest money from the HOF for what became Housing Hope Village (HHV).

Housing Hope Village before and after

To focus attention on fundraising, the Capital Fund Committee partnered with the Knoll Lumber Company of Monroe who had donated a house built for the 1994 Seattle Home Show. The show was held in the Kingdome, and after the show was over, eight local labor unions volunteered to disassemble the house and move it to Kennedy Court. With extra material donated by Knoll, the crew transformed the house into a two-story duplex which would serve two homeless

CONGRATULATIONS
to Housing Hope on the grand opening of
HOUSING HOPE VILLAGE

COMMUNITY OPEN HOUSE
October 25 & 26, 1997
Noon to 5 p.m.
5830 Evergreen Way, Everett

Herald newspaper publicity

families. This won great publicity, as did the ribbon cutting for Self Help Housing's first families to move into their homes - eight at Gold Bar and 16 at Lake Alyson. 24 homes had been built at these two locations, and Housing Hope, at Mae Storks' suggestion, began the tradition of giving each family a rhododendron for their garden along with their house keys. All of these generated publicity and excitement about Housing Hope's work, but the greatest excitement surrounded the largest and most complex project ever undertaken by the agency: the purchase and rehabilitation of the Commerce Building at 1801 Hewitt Avenue in downtown Everett.

The Commerce Building

This was an enormous project. The vacant, five story office building built in 1910 could provide 48 housing units, but at a cost of more than $3,500,000. Everett's original commercial district had died in the 1960s when merchants left for suburban malls that offered free parking. But with better economic times the old downtown was expected to flourish as a financial center, and some investors rushed to purchase its depressed properties before demand increased their value. Within Everett, the derelict Monte Cristo Hotel, once the civic, social and cultural heart of the city, beckoned as a possible site for transitional housing, but Aat considered the Commerce Building, home of William Stockbridge's long abandoned Bank of Commerce, to be a better candidate.

Exploratory moves began as early as 1991 when Housing Hope entered into a joint venture with real estate developer C. J. Ebert, who offered to put down $150,000 in earnest money. As grant and loan proposals were submitted and site control negotiations moved forward, the agency sought a new funding source.

Low-Income Housing Tax Credits

In June of 1993 Ed and Nik Halladay of Housing Hope's Board of Directors attended a dinner meeting in Seattle hosted by the national nonprofit Local Initiatives Support Corporation (LISC). Founded by the Ford Foundation in 1979 to support local creation of affordable housing, LISC (later renamed Impact Capital) provided capital, technical assistance, training and information to community development agencies such as Housing Hope. Capital in the form of equity investments —money—came via the LISC-spawned National Equity Fund, a body that provided a new source of funding: Low-Income Housing Tax Credits (LIHTC).

Commerce Building is over 100 years old (left) in 1910 (right) in 2010

This funding instrument came about as a last-minute deal to assure passage of the Bradley Tax Reform Act of 1986, an effort to simplify the federal tax code, decrease tax rates, close tax loopholes and increase corporate taxes. Because the Bradley Bill reduced investment incentives for rental housing, the LIHTC was hastily added to generate investment in low income housing by crediting tax rebates to groups building low-income rental housing in an amount equal to a percentage—up to 70%—of the cost of the project. This amount could, in turn, be offered through a syndicator such as the National Equity Fund (NEF) to an investing entity that would provide up to a dollar of capital for every dollar of low income tax credit. The project sponsor who would operate the housing received the money and the investing entity received a certificate which informed the IRS that the investing entity's taxes were to be lowered by the credited amount. By giving away potential corporate tax revenues, the government was essentially giving away money. The program became wildly successful, creating some 2,400,000 units of low-income housing in its first 20 years. In the case of the Commerce Building, nearly half of its $3.5 million capital budget came from funds raised by from low-income housing and historic tax credits, although this early into the program's history, investors were only offering 50 cents on the dollar. When large corporations with significant taxes calculated their potential return on investment, some offered slightly more than a dollar per dollar of credit. But as is so often the case, becoming dependent on 'free' money came with its own costs.

Commerce Building Limited Partnership (CBLP)

When underwriters at the NEF, who offered to purchase the tax credits from Housing Hope, looked at Housing Hope's balance sheet, they saw risk and therefore required that a new entity, not Housing Hope, become the General Partner. Again, with legal assistance from tax credit guru Mark Kantor, Housing Hope created a new non-profit entity, Building Credits, to serve as General Partner for any tax credit project Housing Hope undertook with the NEF. To date there have been seven, with the Commerce Building being the first. Mark and his firm have provided invaluable technical assistance for all these entities.

Because Commerce Building Limited Partnership (CBLP) was a for-profit corporation whose financial benefits—in the form of tax credits, depreciation and certain cash flows—were returned to investors, a great deal of discussion took place prior to reaching the consensus needed to approve it. The project was undeniably huge, but the city really wanted the building restored to its former elegance, and 48 low-income housing units became a means to this end. When word of the corporation's desire to replace the building's 157 pivot windows with safer and more energy efficient units became public, however, the Historical Preservation Society weighed in to point out that the pivoting windows, which could be opened to the breeze (when the pulp mills' stench was downwind), was one of the major reasons the building was worth preserving in the first place. The corporation countered that, when the tall windows were open, nothing prevented anyone stepping up to fill their lungs with fresh air from falling to their death on the pavement below, but the preservationists won out. The project was completed with the existing windows repainted, but it would take more than a decade to improve the building's energy efficiency and fully restore the windows to their former glory. The restoration put the building on the National Register of Historic Places and earned Housing Hope a low-income historic tax credit in 1995, then later $700,000 from multiple sources to finish refurbishing the windows. The windows were finally completed in 2010. As to their safety, Housing Hope adopted the view that apparently all previous owners had credited people with enough sense not to fall out of them, and since no one in its 102 year history has, they seem to have been right. When the facility opened in September, 1995 to considerable fanfare, it provided 20 studio apartments, 28 single-occupancy apartments, two community kitchens, three street-front commercial spaces, a building manager's office and a tenant lounge. Twenty-nine of the apartments served homeless individuals who received subsidized rent in partnership with the Everett Housing Authority.

Another Look at the Parable of the Good Samaritan

But 19 of the Commerce Building apartments were not subsidized. These unsubsidized units served individuals with incomes at or below 50% of area median income. Market apartments (residential units rented at a market rate) had been let at Crossroads, the agency's original emergency shelter, and at several subsequent projects, but they became more common as Housing Hope went forward with larger projects. Although the income stream these provided paid down mortgages and supported an ever-increasing need for services to the poor, the agency had to master the difficult financial calculus all social service providers ultimately face. In a wry moment, John Sevy, who we shall meet later, described real estate development as ten minutes of fun followed by 30 years of management. Investors love to see a building take shape: an old structure is covered by scaffolding and emerges new and bright, or foundations are poured, framing rises, walls are painted and a brand new building is celebrated with a ribbon cutting on manicured grounds. But then you're stuck taking care of it, and services go unnoticed except in the lives of receivers. One-time, up-front capital dollars pay for a building, but payments for services never end. And while a building can make money in rents, lifting the poor out of their condition is not a money-maker in the short term. And, as a result, funding construction is a lot easier than funding services.

Tomorrow's Hope van donated by Boeing employees

As Housing Hope had already learned, the services required by homeless individuals are often difficult to provide. As it sought to deal with the problems of homeless families, the agency became, by default, their primary service provider. As we have seen, when no one else in the community stepped up to meet the special needs of children from homeless families, Housing Hope developed Tomorrow's Hope. Beyond the prominent issues of rising rents and child care, the impact on homeless families of catastrophic health issues and job loss exacerbated by incomplete education, drug and alcohol addictions, family violence and family cultures of poverty multiplied the problem. And education was a daunting challenge. In addition to standard academic or professional training, life skills education had to replicate or exceed those that had normally taken place in intact families, where skills in budgeting, scheduling, networking, personal development and strategic planning had become the norm. As this became apparent so did the realization that the previous educational experiences of Housing Hope's clients had often been overwhelmingly negative. For them schools had not been a way out or a way up but a source of constant discomfort, despair and humiliation. The agency's success dealing with these seemingly intractable problems came, in part, from never shying away from them.

Increased understanding affected program development. For example, instead of restricting the program to its own clients, Tomorrow's Hope became the first to offer its services to the children of homeless families served by other providers such as VOA, YWCA, Everett Gospel Mission and the Interfaith Association. The purchase of larger 15-passenger van, made possible by a $23,700 grant from the BEGNF in 1995, made it possible to transport children to and from shelters and Tomorrow's Hope. As each child's issues became better understood, Tomorrow's Hope addressed them.

Parents often had critical educational needs, and these were neither ignored nor passed along to other institutions; in fact, no institution that adequately dealt with them existed. In counseling sessions, motivational questioning helped individuals identify the causes of their homelessness and the strengths and aptitudes they possessed that could be developed to overcome it, and counselors directed them toward classes that addressed these issues.

Service became integral to the agency's mission as it evolved from a housing agency to a Community Development Corporation. The original mission statement was amended to add services: ***"Housing Hope shall promote and provide a continuum of safe, decent and affordable housing and necessary related services for low and very low income residents of Snohomish County and Camano Island".*** No one expected that this would be easy, and they were right. Many attribute the agency's successes to the enormous amount of time and informed exploratory discussion the board devoted to reaching a workable consensus. To make sure recipients themselves would be part of the decision-making process, the board invited several to become board members. Looking back, all board members emphasized, often with amazement, the amount of deliberation every good decision required. But the reality remained that while it was relatively easy to build something, providing adequate services to a struggling population presented a constant challenge. Risk attended everything they did, but as Ed said, they were in the business of risk management, not risk aversion.

More About Low-Income Housing Tax Credits

Following consultant recommendations to enhance its housing development capacity, and with a grant from a very special partner, Impact Capital an affordable housing intermediary lending group, the agency augmented Aat's housing developer job with a full-time housing development director position and hired John Sevy. John, a graduate of the University of Oregon and Scotland's University of Edinburgh's School of Civic Administration, had experience in city planning and administration, and had served as city manager of Carnation, in King County, WA. In 1995, he left his post in Carnation to come to Housing Hope, where he focused on developing and financing low-income housing, which included financing programs with tax credits.

Corporations using low-income housing tax credits are, by definition, for-profits where any profit goes to its owners. This is in stark contrast to non-profits, where a profit is called a surplus and is reinvested in the communities they serve. Increasing the number of poor people served by a project improved the chances for receiving low-income tax credits, but that necessarily increased the need for social services. Fortunately Housing Hope made a wise decision early in its tax credit history. The primary investor selected

Housing Hope's entry wins the first place prize of $3,000 at Gingerbread Jubilee, sponsored by Impact Capital in December 2011

The Impact Capital Story

It was 1994. Housing Hope was seven years old. Impact Capital (IC), the local name for LISC, a national affordable housing intermediary, was interested in helping to build the capacity for affordable housing production in Snohomish County.

Housing Hope had been pestering them for help, so IC did two things. John Berdes, the CEO, felt that Housing Hope needed an experienced housing director capable of accessing equity and debt financing at a larger scale. IC funded the creation of this new position with a startup grant and also funded a consultant to develop a strategic development plan for the organization. This would be useful in convincing funders of the merit of Housing Hope's proposals.

Berdes was succeeded by Tom Lattimore who also became a champion for Housing Hope. Over the years he supported housing predevelopment grants, a five-year capacity building grant aimed at creating and developing a regional delivery system involving branches of Housing Hope in the east and north areas of the county. IC also funded an upgraded technology platform that brought Housing Hope into the modern IT era. In 2012, long time friend of Housing Hope Judith Olsen became the CEO of IC and discussions were launched on continuing and enhancing the partnership.

Also, IC connected Housing Hope with National Equity Fund, a nonprofit tax credit syndicator who became a valuable partner with Housing Hope.

by Housing Hope was the National Equity Fund, which took its profits in the form of tax credits and depreciation, not cash flow.

Housing Hope ultimately developed eleven separate corporations, seven of which received tax credits, all with overlapping board responsibilities. John Sevy likened this to a Viennese torte: each layer made according to a different recipe, whose sous-chefs were overseen by a hard-eyed government chef and all were held together by complex, complicated funding schemes. In the fevered financial environment of the mid-2000s, low-income tax credits and the poor they served became entangled in the world of commoditization; the creation of complex and impenetrable financial instruments that eventually went haywire. Ultimately, the value of low-income tax credits would vanish in the financial collapse of 2008, and tax credit financing for low-income housing dried up. When this happened, Housing Hope landed on its feet because of its close ties to a resilient community, its dedication to financial propriety, and the skills of its lawyers and planners, but for a time it lost an invaluable leveraging tool. As John noted, while the agency typically had three or four projects in progress at any one time before the collapse, in several years following, with the exception of Self Help Housing, it rarely had more than one.

An Internal Debate

Low income tax credits were a feature of the IRS code and did not apply to Self Help Housing, which was funded by grants and loans from the USDA. Because Self Help Housing involved people of modest incomes already employed and with good credit ratings, the USDA could count on stable income streams for repayment of mortgages. The idea of programs enabling plucky low-income people to build their own homes was very attractive, and some wondered whether Housing Hope would shift its focus from those in greatest need to those who could benefit most immediately from a hand up into the world of home ownership.

The issue vexed Todd Morrow. In 1994 he met Ed at the title office, with champagne, to sit at a huge conference table and sign many inches of legal and financial documents, thereby finalizing the purchase of the Commerce Building.

Ed and Todd sign closing documents for Commerce Building tax credits

But Todd believed that the large sums paid the lawyers and accountants (some called them tax credit junkies), hired to make sure the complex tax-credit arrangements were legal, would have been better spent acquiring properties and providing services. Tax credit financing followed an arcane top-down

...After all, can you imagine raising a child without a home or trying to maintain a family life and keep your child safe and healthy while living in a car? For far, far too many families in Snohomish County, this is a fact of daily life. For many other families already at risk because they cannot find affordable housing, it will take only the loss of employment or the illness of the wage earner before this nightmare becomes a reality. Housing Hope offers a hand up, not a hand out. Our services include Tomorrow's Hope which provides daily care for up to 26 homeless children from shelters throughout the county. This allows parents to improve their education and seek employment without worry for their children's well being. Our staff helps families assess their situations, acquire new skills needed to attain self-sufficiency, and return to the community at low risk for future homelessness. Our program for homeless pregnant women, Century House, offers them a place to live while they await the birth of their infants. They also take the opportunity to develop skills and to learn about infant care and parenting. Your donations may mean the difference between a family unraveling as they spend more and more nights in a car, or putting their lives back together and returning to the community as self-sufficient, tax-paying citizens."

– Todd Morrow

business model rather than the collaborative model pioneered at Stanwood and Arlington that drew its support from the people. Would picnics where those serving and those served shared a common, hopeful meal be replaced by celebrations where attorneys toasted bankers?

Late in 1995, Frank McCord offered Housing Hope's board of directors the use of Cascade Bank's conference room, and it was in this plush setting, where members could recline on comfortable chairs around an elegant oak table, that Todd asked the board to reflect upon its mission to serve the poorest of the poor. He had raised similar thoughts at an annual capital fund campaign banquet a few months earlier.

Like fellow board member Greg Provenzano he was a champion for serving the lowest income segment of the community. Todd understood that services were expensive and difficult to fund, but he wanted to make sure that the interests of the very poor would not be ignored in the pursuit of attractive programs and financial complexities. The irony of the boardroom setting was not lost on an audience grappling with the enormous challenges posed by its deceptively succinct mission. In order to provide 'safe, decent and affordable housing and necessary related services' to the low- and very low-income people of the county, Housing Hope needed to deal with the root causes of homelessness and not be co-opted by the powerful financial and governmental entities it relied upon for support. The agency had made great progress dealing with homelessness, but the problem was nowhere near solved. Making use of low income tax credits proved an effective way to build housing, but even if Housing Hope's guests graduated from all the classes they could take during transitional housing, without decent jobs awaiting them where would they go? Free money was a boon, but the primary source of support would always be the local community. And in the effort to realize their mission, Housing Hope had many allies.

The Windermere Foundation

By this time the agency's original emergency shelter, Crossroads, had been remodeled thanks to a $60,000 grant from the Windermere Foundation, founded in 1989 as the philanthropic arm of Windermere Real Estate. When the facility re-opened at a well-attended ribbon-cutting ceremony in April of 1996, it was renamed the Windermere Crossroads Apartments.

Barb Lamoureux, chairperson of the Windermere Foundation Snohomish County office at the time, had been present at the original 1988 ribbon cutting, and had been instrumental in making this generous grant possible. When she discussed how much Windermere Foundation could contribute to the agency, Ed told her that the greatest importance of any contribution was how it could be used it to leverage other grants and funds. Over the years she had developed a strong relationship with Housing Hope and often joked that whenever Ed took her out to lunch to discuss new ideas, it usually ended up costing her about $5,000.

Windermere Real Estate and $60,000 donation

Barb Lamoureux

In 1972, John Jacobi founded Windermere Real Estate in the Seattle neighborhood of the same name, where the company's headquarters are still located.

As his offices proliferated in Seattle, Jacobi encouraged an attitude of community service by promoting a Community Service Day and sponsoring the annual Windermere Cup Crew races in Seattle's Montlake Cut. In 1989, he founded the non-profit Windermere Foundation to fight homelessness, and asked agents to donate $2.50 from every Windermere transaction. These would be channeled to worthy programs.

One of their agents was Barbara Lamoureux, 'an original Everett girl' in her words, born and raised in town and a 1963 graduate of Everett High School, who went to work for Windermere at Mill Creek in 1989. Using her growing voice, Lamoureaux wondered aloud if some of the money agents were collecting for the Foundation, which mostly went to King County, could stay in Snohomish County. She had always remembered her grandfather's advice that one shouldn't take money out of a community to make a living and not pay it back. The company had eleven offices in Snohomish County, and in 1994, the Snohomish County branch of the Windermere Foundation was organized with her as its chair, with the understanding that any donation beyond the $2.50 per transaction would stay in the county. To set an example, she donated $100 per transaction and others followed suit.

Housing Hope sites were located near Windermere offices all through the county. So it made sense to align Windermere's homeless funding with the agency. Barb made sure agents knew where the agency's emergency and transitional housing facilities were located. "This way, they could drive past it themselves, or with their family or a client and say this is where part of their commission goes."

When the Keep Hope Alive million-dollar campaign neared completion after a long year of work in 2000, Barb received a call from Deborah Bolton, Housing Hope's development director, who told her excitedly how close they were to meeting their goal. "How close?" she asked. "We only need to raise $20,000 more." "Well," Barb answered, "The Foundation can cover that; I'll send you a check today". And hearing that, Bolton burst into grateful tears.

Deirdre Kvangnes

Deirdre Kvangnes, Windermere Realtor, has been dubbed "Glinda the Good" by Ed. This came about as a result of Deirdre's bowling team dressed as witches.

With green face and tall pointed hat, she actually resembled the Wicked Witch of Oz, but from Housing Hope's perspective there was nothing but goodness beneath that hat.

Deirdre represented Marysville in the Windermere Foundation program and participated in the donation to refurbish Crossroads. When Barb stepped down from leading Snohomish County Windermere Foundation, Deirdre stepped up as the new chair. She supported the golf tournament, and when Housing Hope opened Beachwood Apartments "she jumped in to support". Annual bowl-a-thons led by Barb and Marysville Windermere colleagues supported the Beachwood service program for homeless families.

Kay, Barb and Deirdre

Her team of Realtors have organized community service day work parties at Beachwood for years. And under her lead the Marysville Rotary Club has been a staunch supporter of Housing Hope. The Windermere Foundation's Over and Above campaign provided the agency with two $100,000 pledges for its ambitious $7 million Build Serve Sustain campaign in 2004 and 2006, the latter to help reach the goal.

Kay Frederickson

When Deirdre stepped down, Glinda the Second stepped up to chair the Windermere Foundation in the county.

Kay Frederickson immediately began strengthening the golf tournament to benefit Housing Hope and secured support of the Mill Creek Rotary Club. Continuing the legacy of her predecessors, she's become a great friend of the agency as she coordinates the countywide Windermere support for Housing Hope's mission.

The Lervick Family Village

As the Crossroads remodel neared completion, work went forward on the Lervick Family Village. A property in Stanwood had been purchased in 1993, and a year later the agency received a $338,000 grant from the State Housing Trust Fund plus two grants from Snohomish County and began construction of a large transitional housing facility with three single-family homes, along with two additional buildings with five apartments each. Five units would provide transitional housing for homeless families, and the other eight would be rented out to low income families. By the time construction began in November 1995, the Stanwood/Camano Action Committee had succeeded in raising $125,000. A major capstone donation from Arne and Ida Lervick covered all remaining construction costs and created an endowment with earnings dedicated to providing services for the agency's Stanwood projects. In 1998, proceeds from the sale of the original emergency shelter house in Stanwood were added to the Stanwood Endowment Fund.

Lervick Family Village ground breaking

Arne Lervick

In 1943 Arne Lervick and brothers, Arthur, Magnar and Ole started Twin City Foods, a frozen vegetables business that enjoyed phenomenal growth after the war.

Steve and Jo Saunders with Arne

Arne became widely regarded as an astute and aggressive businessman, and a man of few words. Arne appreciated his roots in Stanwood and the interdependence of his business with the success of workers from this community, many of whom paid their way through college from summer wages earned at Twin City Foods.

Arne had a long history of charitable support for needs in Stanwood. He supported the bicentennial fireworks and sent the company trucks out when there was a fire or flood. When Housing Hope secured property for its new housing development it approached Arne for support. His simple "sure" provided the final $75,000 of the project's capital budget and the family also seeded an endowment fund with a further $75,000. The new facility which opened in July 1996 was named Lervick Family Village.

Hundreds attended his funeral at Our Savior's church in January, 1998. The family designated memorial gifts in honor of Arne, and later in honor of his wife, Ida, to support Housing Hope's program in Stanwood. Over $25,000 in memorial gifts were received, honoring the family that had helped build the community and saw to it that its most vulnerable citizens would be served long after Arne's passing.

The Arne and Ida Lervick legacy has lived on. Family members Irene Amundsen, Wendy Lervick and Tammy Lervick are involved with the Stanwood Ambassadors who make sure Lervick Family Village continues to thrive.

A Little Light Near The End Of The Tunnel

During the first half of the 1990s the United States enjoyed an extended period of economic growth coinciding with the Presidency of Bill Clinton. During that period 24 million jobs were created; the national unemployment rate fell to around 4%, and Clinton's administration ended with a projected budget surplus. Growth was fueled by advances in information technology, especially in Washington State, the headquarters of Microsoft, Inc., and a major center of the dot-com boom. In those years Washington's population grew by over a million, increasing by more than 21% over the previous decade, more than half due to in-migration primarily to urban areas with nearly half the state's total population living in King, Pierce and Snohomish Counties. In Snohomish County, population growth of around 30% was accompanied by a surge in housing construction, and from 1990 to 1995 the number of people turned away from emergency shelters actually decreased as Housing Hope and other agencies made more low-income housing available.

Self Help Housing: An Update

Although the numbers were small, the agency's Self Help Housing Program had made an impact. By October of '95, the sixteen families of Groups 4 and 5 had moved into their new homes in the Blue Spruce Grove subdivision near Granite Falls, followed in June of '96 by eight more from Group 6. By then 25 lots had been purchased at Smokey Point, a residential area near Arlington, where Groups 7, 8 and 9 began work on their homes in a subdivision known as Timber Park. In July of 1997, five more lots were purchased at the Lake Shores subdivision at Lake Howard, northeast of Everett, for Group 10.

Self Help Housing families hard at work

The Teen Parent Housing Council

The state's economic growth in manufacturing, in the number of manufacturing firms and in wages peaked around 1995-96, but declined sharply with the dot-com bust, and the nation was in recession by 2001. Disturbingly, throughout this period, the largest group in poverty remained unmarried women with children, and in Snohomish County, the youngest of these began showing up in unexpected places.

Lake Stevens, a small community east of Everett on the northeast shore of the lake, began as a lumber mill like its larger neighbor, but with the big trees gone it billed itself as a sport fishing resort and a place to get away from it all. A residential community developed, incorporating itself in 1960 to preserve its non-commercial character. If some complained it lacked excitement, jobs or services, which could be had five miles away in Everett, others touted its charms as a laid-back, bedroom community. But when an increasing number of unmarried teens ended up getting pregnant, concerned citizens took note. In Everett, a young, unmarried pregnant woman who had been ejected by her family could go to Cocoon House, established by therapist Sarri Gilman in 1991, or Century House, but in Lake Stevens, if there were not kin to take her in, she would have to hang ten on a davenport of a friend. She could go to Everett, but the idea of a Lake Stevens mother-to-be having to leave school and migrate to Everett's mean streets gave many pause.

1997 Christmas card

Nancy Mobley, who worked in local real estate, had mentored teens in need and gathered data on homeless teen parents. In 1992 she talked several people she knew into volunteering to create a new non-profit which they named Teen Parent Housing Council (TPHC). Funding applications for a teen parent housing facility were submitted to Snohomish County and the state, and in 1995 Avanti House, with two 2-two bedroom apartments for homeless mothers separated by a community room, was constructed and opened.

Volunteers agreed to staff the house, which had an upstairs apartment for a Resident Manager, who sometimes doubled as a house mother. Teen mothers 16 to 18 years old could stay for up to two years as long as they attended school or until they graduated. They would be helped to find work, which might require a bus trip to Everett, but their babies would be cared for, and, when able, they could pay a small rent. Rules were strict: residents had to stay in school;

there was a 10:00 PM curfew every night, no alcohol or drugs were permitted on site, and no smoking was permitted inside. Typically poor at relationships, each young woman had a roommate, and they could help each other learn. Instructors were brought in to teach life skills, and a case manager was provided along with a nurse as needed. Needless to say, with unmarried teen pregnancy a growing problem, there was always a waiting list.

The Lake Stevens Action Committee, 1997

Bob Craven, a Lake Stevens Rotarian and local insurance company owner, and Marie Campbell, a seasoned human services professional joined in Mobley's work as founding board members. Terri Spencer, Joyce Bell and other prominent Lake Stevens leaders also joined the board. Bob Craven was joined in 1997 by his wife, Cathy. Margi Layman, who volunteered as a landscaper, ended up becoming a member of the Council board. Their work was well supported and inspiring, but also exhausting since it was a board-run operation. In addition, teaching female adolescents to grow up and adequately care for their children was complicated. The young mothers were totally devoted to their children, most of the time, but without an education, life skills, income, parental support and with a baby in tow at all times - managing the house was a constant challenge. When a boyfriend brought a gun into the house, the TPHC board realized they needed help. With no administrative staff or manager to oversee operations, reporting and compliance, they began looking for an umbrella organization to provide needed support and to give the program renewed focus. Bob - the board president - and Marie contacted Housing Hope in 1996. Knowing that grassroots support was the key to Housing Hope's successful model, Ed agreed to recommend approval of a merger to the Housing Hope board, but on one condition: he asked Bob to stay involved. However, tough negotiator that he was, Bob offered his wife Kathy instead. On January 1, 1997, after extended discussions, the TPHC became a subsidiary of Housing Hope and a Lake Stevens Action Committee was formed based on the model of Stanwood and Arlington. Margi, the landscape volunteer, was destined to play a prominent role for the next nine years. She ended up becoming a member of the Housing Hope board. When Margi asked Ed who the Council's leader should be, he looked at her with his quizzical smile and said, 'You're it!' As the acknowledged leader, she was quickly elected President. The Teen Parent Housing Council retained its separate nonprofit status for seven years, with Margi as its president throughout. During these years, the agency was able to access United Way grants and to secure Community Development Block Grant funding. In 2004, its separate nonprofit status had served its purpose. TPHC was dissolved and it merged with Housing Hope.

New Century Village

With agreement from First Presbyterian Church, who had donated funds to make Century House possible, it was decided to sell Century House on Everett Avenue and dedicate the proceeds to a new teen parent facility. This enabled the agency to replace a house donated by Grady Helseth with a ten-unit complex to be called New Century House, honoring First Presbyterian's original $50,000 centennial challenge grant. It opened in 2002, providing transitional housing for four women - homeless teen mothers with babies, or pregnant teens - in two apartments. Over time, this would grow to become another village, the 44-unit New Century Village, with 21 apartments sheltering homeless teen moms. This allowed these desperate teenagers to take advantage of a tailored Housing Hope program designed to address their needs. And a play room there, 'Grady's Place,' became a much loved feature, honoring Grady Helseth's support and generosity.

Grady's Place

In the late 1990s, Grady Helseth, a charmingly crusty Everett developer, was donating the use of a house he owned at 2505 Howard in south Everett's Pinehurst neighborhood to Housing Hope, to be used to provide affordable housing.

His mother, Benita, a member of the Mothers' Committee for Action and the League of Women Voters, had always wanted her son to become more involved in social issues, and he grew to appreciate the agency's work. Once while he and Ed were discussing the possible expansion of the facility, an eight-year-old girl walked up to Ed and asked, "Are you Mr. Petersen?" "Yes." "You don't remember me," she continued, "but you got a home for me and my mom last year." Helseth felt his heart melt, and he decided to donate the property. "It was like a movie script," he recalled, "I accused Ed of orchestrating it." And to reward his generosity, the feds gave him—what else?—a tax break.

More Dismal Statistics

The decline of the national, regional and local economy during the latter half of the 1990s was not matched by a concomitant decrease in housing prices, and the number of homeless increased. The yearly count of those turned away from Snohomish County's crowded shelters tells the grim tale. In 1990 a total of 9,206 were turned away; by 1994, that number had dropped to 6,602. There were only 33 more in '95, but then it skyrocketed to 9,286 in '96, 12,099 in '97, 13,120 in '98, and 14,038 in '99, a 111.5% increase in five years, most of whom were families with children, and nearly 20% of whom had been evicted.

An eviction notice stays on a person's apartment rental record for seven years. "What's wrong with us?" a tearful homeless mother asked a newspaper reporter. She was single with four children; she worked hard, followed all the rules, but she and her children had only $50 to survive on after they paid the monthly rent, not enough to live on, and certainly not enough to buy the lawnmower the landlord demanded she purchase in order to cut the lawn. When she could not, they were evicted. "What's wrong with us?" she demanded to know. "I never knew how people got started to live on the streets" wrote another young Everett mother. "But now I know because more than likely in April my kids and my boyfriend will be out living on the streets. I found myself a great job, only part time, but I had to quit because it would hurt our welfare check. So we are poor people that no one wants to rent to because we are on welfare. Could the rich people please tell us what to do beside live on the streets?"

The Marysville Action Committee, 1997

Again, like in Lake Stevens, the homeless began showing up in places they hadn't before. In Marysville, Pastor Rudolph Rowe of the United Methodist Church took notice when homeless families began showing up two or three times a month asking for help. He could point them toward the Bethany Shelter in Everett and the Tulalip House of Prayer on the nearby Tulalip Indian Reservation that his congregation supported, "but," he said, "they've got to leave our town; and that doesn't seem right. We should be taking care of people here." Other pastors and many local citizens agreed, and they asked to meet with Housing Hope. Again the Stanwood Action Committee came to tell their story with support from Arlington and Lake Stevens.

Zoe Hallgren

In January, 1997, a newly organized Marysville Action Committee began meeting to plan for an affordable housing development for low-income households and homeless families. Zoe Hallgren, one of the early members, soon found herself a leader of the committee and on the Housing Hope Board of Directors. The committee began an aggressive fundraising campaign, and Zoe, referred to with some trepidation as the 'Mother of Marysville,' was not above cornering anybody she could find, including board members, and making them sign pledge cards.

Pastors Vic Rodriguez of Marysville Free Methodist and Jack Richards of Bethlehem Lutheran organized Thanksgiving eve services with offerings for Housing Hope to benefit the homeless in this new Marysville project. Housing Hope would use the $100,000 the committee raised to leverage grants and loans to pay the project's estimated two-million-dollar cost. If it seemed a Rube-Goldberg financial scheme to some, Ed assured them that it was "not a half-baked idea; it's at least three-quarters baked." In November the agency purchased property on Beach Avenue at 10th Street for the Beachwood project that would have 25 two- and three- bedroom apartments, five of which were set aside as transitional housing for homeless families and an additional five units for families with a disabled member, especially those with mental disabilities. Pastor Jack Richards was Zoe's pastor, who (probably from Zoe's insistence) had become active in the development campaign. He oversaw a ground-breaking ceremony in April of 1998 at the same time that the organization celebrated not just the beginnings of Beachwood, but also work on 29 lots purchased at Smokey Point where Groups 11 through 14 began constructing their sweat equity homes in Country Manor II.

Beachwood Apartments in Marysville

By February of 1999, Beachwood was ready for a ribbon-cutting. The remarkable success of Housing Hope had become well-enough known that the following year Washington State's Governor, Gary Locke, combined a visit to Marysville's 10th Street School for a chance at a great photo-op. He donned a carpenter's belt, walked across the street with twenty other officials, including county executive Bob Drewel, and helped fence in a play enclosure at Beachwood.

County Executive Drewel, Governor Locke and Ed

Back at the school, Locke told 150 middle schoolers that his family lived in public housing until he was about six years old.

"...That public housing gave my parents enough money after working six, seven days a week, 12 hours a day to save so they could get their own house, and that's the American dream—home ownership. And that's what transitional housing and these low-income housing projects are trying to do—provide people the temporary assistance they need to get back on their feet and pursue the American dream."

– Governor Gary Locke

Locke was no stranger to swinging a hammer or wearing a carpenter's belt, and his straight-forward desire to engage in actual work and his unassuming manner would later enthrall Chinese audiences when this first Asian-American Executive of King County, state governor and Ambassador to The People's Republic of China, and his family were observed walking through Beijing airport carrying their own luggage like normal people rather than have a bevy of obsequious staff members fetch and carry as though he was some cosseted mandarin. At the Beachwood Apartments site, Locke felt quite at home.

Housing Hope Village

By then Housing Hope was comfortably situated in its new offices at Housing Hope Village. Like other projects, HHV took years to develop and it was complicated. Environmental regulations required that a 50-foot buffer be fenced off as a protected area on both sides of Pigeon Creek, with strictly limited development beyond. As a good steward the agency removed non-native plants and monitored the flora afterward. A large retention pool to collect and filter run-off from the roofs and parking lots was constructed.

Childrens book written for Tomorrow's Hope children who play by Pigeon Creek

Ultimately, 17 different local departments had to weigh in before the project could be completed. Local concern about homeless people in the nearby homeowners' back yards required adroit diplomacy. Jessica Barkell, who lived next door to the site, quickly fell in love with the Housing Hope mission and became a staunch advocate in the neighborhood and a volunteer at the agency's reception desk. When one neighbor expressed her concern about how the project might affect the area's slugs, Aat took the time to visit her home, admire her slugs and assure her that as the work progressed, the agency would do all it could to protect the hideous mollusks.

Jim Braun, an Edmonds real estate broker, who led the Building Hope capital fund drive, received help from two prominent bankers. Bob Dickson, the founder of Frontier Bank, and Frank McCord who took turns, in Jim's words, 'browbeating the bankers' at 15 county banks to lock in their support of the project and give it credibility. This smoothed the path to an August meeting with representatives of the State Housing Assistance Program and the State Housing Finance Commission who gave provisional approval for $714,000. In turn, HUD matched this with a five-year, $1,000,000 Supportive Housing Grant for operating costs and services. Ed described the leveraging as "a complex funding matrix, basically a patchwork quilt of city, county, state and federal grants for various pieces of our dream, all with different strings attached." Such financial wizardry may have prompted Connie Niva, earlier a member of the Everett City Council, to say, when she was nominated for a position on Housing Hope's Board of Directors in 1996 and chose as her board responsibility membership in the Finance Committee; that she did so to find out "why we weren't in jail". It should be noted that a reassured Connie continued on the board and served as president from July of 2001 to June of 2004. Funding for the village was finalized by December 1995, and Housing Hope celebrated an inspiring tenth anniversary in the unfinished basement of the nearly-completed complex in September of 1997.

Tenth anniversary gathering of current and past board members

By October, 19 apartments, 13 of which were for homeless families, were ready for occupancy. Thanks to a $133,000 grant to complete the fundraising, facilitated by Dottie Piasecki of the Providence Hospital Mission Fund and delivered by Board President Janice Henning, Tomorrow's Hope excitedly moved into its new space on the first floor. And the agency began filling up its offices.

Another of Connie's many contributions was her determination that Housing Hope take better care of its properties. During its early years Housing Hope seldom had funding for replacement reserves, and cash flow from housing homeless and very low-income families did not exist. The organization relied heavily on volunteers, and while many older buildings had been remodeled, they were other older buildings with an ever-growing catalog of problems typical of any fixer-upper. A leaky roof can be patched, but ultimately it will need replacing. Moreover, tenants sometimes let a lawn go uncut and gardens get weedy, and when the greensward around Century House began to resemble a canebrake, neighbors complained so loudly that Roy Yates and several other members of First Presbyterian's congregation came regularly to mow the lawns. As the need-to-do list grew, Connie felt obligated to say that she would not vote for another project until the agency took better care of what it had. After the four-year Building Hope Capital Campaign, which seemed to go on forever, was completed in '98, attention was turned to raising funds for property upkeep. And in just one year, from 1999 to 2000, The Keep Hope Alive capital replacement fund drive raised one million dollars.

Keep Hope Alive Co-Chairs Ross & Judy Rettenmier (left) and Bob & Margaret Bavasi (right)

SHOP

Despite increased local job opportunities that came toward the end of the '90s, people earning median income in the county, which by then averaged around $47,000, found it more difficult to rent, much less buy a home. The Puget Sound region had become the eighth most expensive real estate market in the United States, and Washington one of the most expensive for rentals, with the three Puget Sound counties of King, Pierce and Snohomish Counties having the highest costs and lowest vacancy rates. Beset by increasing need, the agency kept building at a rapid pace. Self Help Housing received a boost in August of 1998 when it received a $217,000 land acquisition loan from the non-profit Housing Assistance Council (HAC), a New York program that assisted rural communities across the nation, through a program called Self Help Homeownership Opportunity Project (SHOP).

SHOP came about as an amendment to the federal Housing Opportunity Extension Act of 1996, and was administered by HUD. It was a response to a proposal for federal funding made by Habitat for Humanity, a self-described 'Christian Housing Ministry,' originating in Americus, Georgia, whose best known proponent is President Jimmy Carter. SHOP provided grants to purchase lots for sweat equity housing units. Congress also funded HAC, which provided loans of $10,000 per lot to purchase lots for single-family Self Help Housing units. Housing Hope created a revolving loan program in partnership with HAC in 2000, and used the HAC loans to help purchase or develop property. When families from builder groups purchased their finished house from Housing Hope, the same money could be used again to purchase more land, and HAC would forgive the loans after ten years. These internally controlled funds significantly enhanced Housing Hope's own predevelopment funds for new housing development.

Odds and Ends

In 1999 eight lots were purchased for Group 15 at Highland View near Arlington and, a year after that, ten for Group 16 at Bogart Meadows near Granite Falls. In the fall of 1999 two single-family homes and a commercial lot were acquired from the Jenkins family in Stanwood for future growth, and the non-profit Vision Special Needs Housing agency turned over a residence they owned near Frontier Village (Lake Stevens) to Housing Hope to be used for affordable housing. After property was purchased in 1998 at Oakes Avenue in downtown Everett just south of the county courthouse, the agency formed the for-profit Oakes Limited Partnership to receive low-income tax credits for construction. When Oakes Avenue Commons, a 20-unit permanent housing cooperative, opened in July of 2000, 20 low-income families moved in.

As this building went forward, Housing Hope enhanced its child services with the $70,000 HUD Vouch for Children grant for serving homeless children. This McKinney grant, the only 100% service grant awarded in the county, made it possible for other agencies to place homeless children in Tomorrow's Hope and for Housing Hope to place them in other daycare facilities if families lived too distant. In 1999, Housing Hope was asked by the Healthy Communities initiative led by United Way, to be the local Sponsor for the Basic Health Plan in Snohomish County. This program provided uninsured adults with basic health insurance for the next 12 years.

Redux: New Presidents and Programs

The 1990s had been a wild ride, but the agency could look back on a decade of solid achievement and effective organization. Carol Jensen, one of the original members of the Stanwood/Camano Action Committee, succeeded Todd Morrow as president of the board in July, 1996. Margi Layman, who had earned the good-natured title "Queen of Teens", became president of the Teen Parent Housing Council board, serving from 1997 to 2004. In 1998, when Mark Samuelson became president, smooth leadership transitions had become a norm for the board. And migration to new offices - from the Crossroads apartment to the Wetmore office to the Fulton office to the Jeld-Wen bayside office, constantly packing and unpacking in someone else's old space–ended with the opening of the new offices at HHV. With adequate and appropriate workspace, the agency became even more effective. One person who helped make this possible was Mel Southwick, owner of Alternative Telecommunications in Everett. Since 1988 Mel had been a friend and supporter of the Housing Hope program and had donated his expertise over and over. Now, finally, with enough money in the Housing Hope Village capital budget, they could actually pay him to install a state-of-the art telephone and internet

Mel the Phone Guy

Housing Hope had just purchased the Crossroads apartments and wanted to set up an office in one of the eleven apartments. Help was needed and Ed knew Mel Southwick from his days at Mental Health Services, Inc.

Mel & Debbie Southwick

Maybe they were destined to collaborate, as it turns out that Mel and Ed had the same birthday and were born the same year. There was no money to pay Alternative Telecommunications, but Mel agreed to donate the installation of a phone system in apartment number 6.

From that day, Mel has been caught in the Housing Hope spider web. He missed out on the first year of Housing Hope, but for 24 years, whenever Housing Hope has needed phone assistance at five office locations and multiple housing and program sites, Mel Southwick has been there. He has installed and maintained phone systems, providing options for cost containment, securing and installing donated products and advising on phone system development everywhere Housing Hope has gone.

"If Mel isn't nominated for sainthood, he may be voted volunteer of the quarter-century" says Ed, his apparent twin.

system in the new facility. Being interconnected in the same complex meant that staff could call one another with ease and convene meetings in a meeting room at the drop of a hat. The close proximity of key program staff solidified their ability to coordinate their planning, problem-solve challenging situations, and build program infrastructure. Creative and "out of the box" solutions could be fostered in all recesses of this new home. The serendipitous discovery of new ways to solve a problem was enhanced and this helped Housing Hope realize its mission.

Photo courtesy of Justin Best / The Herald

Don Packard cleans the windows at Housing Hope in Everett
April 1, 1999

Commerce Cleaners, 1998

Housing Hope's creative problem-solving skills frequently came in handy. For example, the agency had hired and trained resident managers from its pool of residents to help guests live in quality living environments. Construction supervisors at Self Help Housing developments taught homebuilders the skills they needed to build a house. Eventually someone came up with the idea that individuals trained in maintenance skills might get jobs cleaning downtown offices. VISTA volunteers Shawn Farrell, Jennifer Farrell (not related) and Pegge Nelson provided leadership designing and implementing a program called Commerce Cleaners, which trained individuals in light maintenance, janitorial skills and the use of specialized cleaning products. By contracting them out at minimum wage, it was hoped that trainees could develop a job history for future reference. In 1998, a $35,000 grant from the Medina Foundation made possible the renovation of the Commerce Building's basement to house the program and there were high hopes that the Commerce Cleaners could provide pathways toward full employment. "It is a stepping stone," said Ed Petersen; "That's all some folks need to get started again".

But coming up with a good idea and developing an effective program were two different things. At this point in its history the agency did not yet have the management team in place to ensure that Commerce Cleaners functioned effectively. When one person sent out to clean apartments hurt her back carrying heavy equipment on stairs, there was no one trained to replace her. Because of such 'thinness', the program withered, but the idea was not forgotten. Once Housing Hope created sufficient program infrastructure a decade later, the idea reappeared as HopeWorks Social Enterprises, but this was a program for the new millennium.

Oakes Avenue Commons, 2000

Oakes Avenue Commons was another program that didn't fully make it off the ground as conceived. Five apartments were dedicated to the disabled, with priority given to individuals with mental disabilities. The Common's three buildings with a combined total of 20 apartments were planned as a cooperative to give low-income tenants the experience of running a business. Where Housing Hope typically leased units to individuals, in this case it leased the Commons to the Oakes Avenue Commons Cooperative that then leased units to its members. Cooperatives were Ed's forte, but the low-income housing tax credits financing caused a problem. The State Housing Finance Commission allocated tax credits through criteria and a complex point system for funding awards that was

Oakes Ave Commons (top)
Residents at ribbon cutting (bottom)

quite daunting. Larger counties with more low-income population received more points than other smaller counties, giving King County a competitive edge over Snohomish County. To get more points one could add more low-income residents to the mix – more tenants earning less than 30% of median income wage increased the number of points – but doing so greatly reduced the income stream. These very low-income households, with marginal financial and management skills at best, were put in charge of running a co-op. And their need for expensive support, services and technical assistance was very high.

The co-op's annual budget was $100,000, and the agency sought ways to help it be self-sufficient. Would an outside management agency be hired to do repairs and maintain the grounds or could the co-op do it? Having the co-op do it would involve more hassles than contracting out, but it would cost much less. Ed maintained a brave optimism.

> ***...Part of our challenge is to teach them what is involved in the decision making process, everything from how to read legal documents to organizing meetings and resolving conflicts. We assured them we would provide the mentoring they need and would ease into this. They won't have responsibility they can't handle. What we're trying to accomplish is a solution to homelessness. The more they have these kinds of skills, the more they can negotiate their personal affairs and maintain their housing stability and never become homeless."***
>
> – Ed Petersen

But many of these households were trapped in poverty partly because they did not have these skills, and they were not the kind that could be learned in a classroom setting. Most had no family resources to rely on, and with no net rental income from the project, management services and case workers ultimately had to be financed by fundraising and loans. John Sevy claimed that in order to get low-income tax credits, Housing Hope often had to over-promise service projects that sucked every dime out of rents that were needed to manage the property and pay mortgages. For seven years the agency struggled to make the co-op work, but it proved too expensive to run and it was eventually dissolved. Low-income tax credits might be 'free money,' but in this case they defeated Housing

The Klabunde Factor

Board Member Emeritus Dick Klabunde (1997-2006) has his name etched in the annals of Housing Hope history. Dick served on the Finance Committee for years. He teamed up with Connie Niva to manage the new Keep Hope Alive Endowment investment until the $1 million fund balance was achieved, at which time they celebrated the success and then gladly led the process of selecting a professional investment management firm, Merrill Lynch.

Dick Klabunde

Every year as the Finance Committee reviewed budgets Dick provided fiscal analysis and attention to detail at a level never seen before in the agency. His attention to detail and scrutiny of personnel costs thereafter became known as the "Klabunde Factor".

The Sievers Story

As a teacher Mary Sievers gained awareness of barriers to learning for children without stable housing and homes. She brought these insights to Housing Hope in 1998 as a new board member particularly how the agency created family and child solutions. During her 9 years on the board she helped the agency keep both mission and business balanced. The exuberance over acquiring and constructing more buildings was always tempered by Mary's focus on the families and the children being housed. She served (and still serves) on the board's services committee and provided ongoing advocacy for wrapping effective service programs around the housing developments. Mary has helped raise funds with a special interest in the child development initiative. As a board member emeritus Mary has continued to find innumerable ways to support the mission since graduating off the board in 2007.

Mary Sievers

Hope's efforts to give low-income tenants management experience. But the agency learned over time and adapted to make each project meet real needs, and in fact many success stories occurred at Oakes. Loria Preston who served as the first President of the Oakes Coop went on to eventually achieve her goal of home ownership and later became a valued and effective member of the Housing Hope staff.

As the complexity of financial management grew, an expert team of board members assumed leadership of the finance committee. Fred Safstrom served as treasurer with Connie Niva and Dick Klabunde on his committee. Their job was to review financial reports monthly, oversee audits, manage investments and recommend fiscal policies. In coordination with operations director Steve Gadd and accounting directors Dave Hansard and Carol Williams, this team helped Housing Hope achieve excellence.

Chapter 5 Into The New Millennium: 2000-2007

The Housing Consortium of Everett and Snohomish County

By 2000, Housing Hope had grown and developed to the point where it had helped frame the county's low-income housing agenda, and Ed served as a significant leader in this process. In the early '90s, four agencies - Senior Services, Housing Hope, the Everett Housing Authority and the Housing Authority of Snohomish County - developed the vast majority of low income housing in the county. County Executive Bob Drewel hired a very effective staffer, Marjorie Hite who, out of her passion for affordable housing, convened meetings where executives from each agency regularly got together to share ideas and to plan. This Housing Stakeholders group worked quite well, but when Hite left and took the energy that kept the meetings going with her, Ed suggested the four groups come together as one to advocate more effectively for low-income housing. They agreed to form a new 501(c)3 agency, drew up by-laws, created membership fees and in 2002, hired Susan Millan as the executive director of the Housing Consortium of Everett and Snohomish County (HCESC), with Ed serving as president for the first three years.

June Robinson, Rep. Mike Sells, Governor Gregoire and Ed

It worked to improve communications between municipalities, to lobby the state legislature on housing issues and to host conferences where groups could share information about affordable housing. In 2007, it drew up the Housing Within Reach affordable housing production plan for Snohomish County. The key element was a plan to leverage $5 million in annual local housing funds over ten years into a $1 BILLION program involving more than $50 million in private, state and federal funding investments to dramatically increase the county's supply of affordable low income housing.

The Fortune Family Foundation

In 2000, fortune smiled on Housing Hope quite literally when the agency gained the attention of the Fortune Family Foundation. This local foundation, headquartered in Kirkland, Washington, was founded in 1998 by Cay Fortune and her husband, John Shimer, formerly a professional fundraising specialist.

Cay Fortune

Both understood how difficult life could be for those most at risk in society, especially women and children, and in order to leverage their foundation resources to have maximum impact, they researched and chose groups they thought best served the population they cared about and offered to instruct them in how to dramatically raise revenues from other philanthropic sources. The goal was for groups to turn every dollar provided by the foundation into four dollars of additional revenue from other sources.

Shortly after their foundation was established, Housing Hope's mission, leadership and track record caught their attention, and in April of 2001, after several interviews and meetings, they provided the agency $3,500 to hire the Alford Group, a consulting firm specializing in nonprofits, to build its fundraising capacity. When it became clear that better staffing was needed, it granted $320,000 over four years to establish Annual Giving Manager and Major Gifts Manager positions. Later, when the organization was contemplating a capital campaign, John guided the discussion through the question of feasibility analysis and eventually offered a grant to pay for a good part of the feasibility study if the board would step up, contribute, and provide leadership. John believed a video and speakers bureau was needed for Housing Hope to better tell its very compelling story. Once a good plan was formulated the Fortune Family Foundation funded the production of a video and the equipment needed for the speaker's bureau.

An outcome of all this was to transform the intimate Stone Soup dinners into an annual signature fundraising event. The dinners always were and would be free in the same way that Ed treated Barb Lamoureux to lunch at their meetings. Henceforth guests would be asked to bring friends and associates, especially those with a heart for the issue and the means to contribute, to make a spontaneous contribution. Ed gave the dinner's keynote address and often called on those who had benefited from Housing Hope's programs to speak, but the new highlight would be the 'ask,' when all present were asked to consider what they could give to help Housing Hope carry out its mission. When Shimer suggested that $100,000 could be raised at such a dinner, Ed was, in his own words, 'completely blown away'.

After all, these had started as humble potlucks, and there was some hesitancy about turning what had been a thank you to contributors into a fundraiser, but Connie Niva, who in the past had encouraged Housing

Shimer and Philanthropy

John Shimer

John Shimer had an itch to teach. His wife Cay Fortune had an itch to make a difference. Together they created the Fortune Family Foundation and committed to seeking out a few worthy charities to support.

Housing Hope didn't find them; John found Housing Hope and offered to help. His career in fundraising positioned him to understand best practices and he systematically approached each funding decision with the clear mission of teaching the agency how to position first its request, and then the funding, for success.

John Shimer was the most engaged funder Housing Hope has ever experienced. He gave of his time, making many trips to Everett to learn, discuss and befriend. He gave of his talent with advice and teaching. His contributions over a span of ten years have dramatically strengthened Housing Hope's impact on homelessness.

Hope to think in grander terms, thought that in light of its new purpose the dinners - which had featured juice and soft drinks - needed sprucing up. "You're going to bilk them out of their money," she jibed, "would it kill you to offer them wine, and NOT in a plastic cup?" The constant repetition of the word 'hope' in Hope Builders, Tomorrow's Hope, Building Hope, the College of Hope, Keep Hope Alive and HopeWorks was another of her pet peeves, but taking her cue, the 2001 dinner, hosted in the shell of the former Peking Duck restaurant immediately south of Housing Hope's offices, generated an astonishing $60,000. The $110,000 that the 'ask' generated in 2004 proved Shimer had been right, but he blew Ed away again by predicting they would ultimately bring in $250,000. Inspired by Shimer's belief in Housing Hope, the 2012 dinner brought in a net total of $254,000.

Stone Soup 2003 at Event Center

In 2003, the Fortune Family Foundation provided $30,000 for a feasibility study to plan the agency's Build, Serve, Sustain comprehensive capital campaign. Based on feasibility study results, consultants advised that $4.5 million could be raised. Sensing what was out there and leveraging a $1.4 million grant from the Bill and Melinda Gates Foundation, the board proposed a goal of $6.9 million. But who would lead such an audacious initiative? Two long-standing supporters with lots of chutzpah stepped up to the task. Long-time board member and former president of the board Connie Niva, and banker John Dickson, CEO of Housing Hope's banking partner Frontier Bank, agreed to serve as co-chairpersons. John was the son of long-time champion and supporter Bob Dickson. Funds raised were for the development of 270 housing units at 8 locations together with services for homeless families and funds to sustain and endow the program. The campaign, which commenced in 2004 and ended in 2006, ultimately raised $7 million, the third largest campaign result ever in the county.

Build, Serve, Sustain Co-Chairs Connie Niva and John Dickson "hit the ball out of the park"

Alongside Fortune, Windermere and Gates Foundations were four other charitable foundations that embraced the Housing Hope mission. Several multi-year grants were instrumental in building the agency's capacity in key areas. EverTrust, led by executive director Mary Sievers, a Housing Hope Board Member Emeritus, funded the development of Tomorrow's Hope childcare and later the economic empowerment initiative. Whitehorse Foundation embraced and funded both the College of Hope development and Tomorrows Hope and more recently the economic empowerment project. Medina Foundation, a strong champion for a basic needs

Connie Niva

Connie Niva grew up on comfortable Rucker Hill in Everett, but her parents knew what hard times were, and frequently told her and her siblings that they were but one step away from the poor house.

Connie Niva

Even though all went to college, they were told in no uncertain terms that "there would be no going to get a degree in English!" They were to get substantial degrees to make sure they could always take care of themselves. In 1967 she graduated from Western Washington University in microbiology and chemistry.

Connie became a leader in Everett. In 1986 she was elected to the City Council. Constantly engaged in community affairs, she served as chair of the Washington State Transportation Commission, was elected to the Everett Port Commission, selected as a Regent of Washington State University, and has served on many boards. Of all the these, however, she unabashedly says that Housing Hope remains her favorite.

Few people get to the heart of the matter as quickly as Connie. She asks hard questions and forces the right conversations to happen. During Connie's nine years on the board the organization grew dramatically. Three successful capital campaigns, the partnership with Gates Foundation, five new tax credit entities all were successful under her watch. She served as President of the board and co-chaired the $7 million Build Serve Sustain campaign. Connie continues to respond whenever Housing Hope needs her sage involvement.

safety net, assisted many of the agency's new projects over a twenty year period. And the Everett Clinic Foundation, the employer of Housing Hope founding board member Jon Witte, also provided grants for virtually every new major initiative of the agency.

The Housing Hope East Snohomish County Branch, 2003

With population growth in the county, citizens had travelled further and further into the outlying areas of the county to find affordable places to live, far away from their workplaces. The housing shortage that became an issue in Everett and in urban and suburban areas also affected rural communities in the Skykomish River valley along Highway 2. Housing costs increased, which led predictably to an increase in homelessness. Sharon Tuohy, of the East Snohomish County VOA program, hoped affordable housing developers could be enticed eastwards to fill the need. "One of the stressors here is, first, the timber industry crashed. Now there's Welfare to Work. There's folks living up in the valley who don't want to go into urban areas and don't ask for assistance until they're in crisis."

A volunteer group, the Sky Valley Homeless Task Force, had met regularly since 1998 in Monroe and worked with churches and other groups to develop an emergency shelter, but it had no real success. There was no affordable housing program east of the city of Snohomish. In the fall of 2002 Ed was asked to consult with individuals planning a new non-profit affordable housing agency for east Snohomish County. There were six members of this group: Marilyn Komnick, a community activist; Martin Boyle, the superintendent of the Index School District; Veronica Haywood, a realtor with Preview Properties; Nick Straley, an attorney with Columbia Legal Services; Jay Randall, a single dad with children who had experienced homelessness; and Tony Balk, a community organizer of long experience hailing from New Jersey, who became the group's first president.

TOWNS

Herald Monday, February 23, 2004 B3

Housing Hope looks east

Group buys in Sultan to bring affordable housing to the area

BY YOSHIAKI NOHARA
Herald Writer

MICHAEL V. MARTINA / The Herald

A five-unit apartment at 519 Fourth St. in Sultan is now in the hands of Housing Hope. As the current tenants leave, Housing Hope will rent units to low-income county residents.

Life turned grim for Robert Harrison when Boeing laid off the assembly line electrician in 2000.

His monthly paycheck of about $3,600 was gone. Harrison, his wife, Lori, and their children, Tyler and Shalynn, had to move out of their place in Mukilteo, ending up in a tent in friend's backyard in Stanwood.

Harrison went from job to job, but kept getting laid off.

Now, Harrison is still jobless, but things have dramatically improved.

He is learning computer science at Edmonds Community College to get a good-paying job in the future. With his wife disabled, the only family monthly income is $950 that the military pays Harrison for school.

But the family lives in a three-bedroom apartment in Marysville for $50 per month, thanks to Housing Hope, an Everett-based nonprofit organization.

"(The low-income housing) built a more stable environment for the entire family," Harrison, 31, said, adding that Tyler, 10, and Shalynn, 8, don't need to worry about where they're going to sleep at night or switching to a different school any more.

Harrison said he knows many homeless families are struggling all over Snohomish County. And Housing Hope now will be able to help families like the Harrisons in Sultan, as it bought two properties for affordable housing there for $520,000 in January. The first property is a five-unit housing complex at 519 Fourth St. ...

... house will be rented to families with 50 percent or less of area median income. A typical tenant would likely be a family of four, earning about $20,000 annually, Bolton added.

The group also will build 10 units of affordable rental housing on a 1-acre vacant lot near the first property, Bolton said. Four units will be temporary housing for homeless families. Construction is likely to start late this year.

The group will try to keep the two properties affordable for at least 40 years, Bolton said.

Those who live in the temporary housing will receive assistance, such as career advice, to overcome homelessness, said Tony Balk, a board director of Housing Hope.

"It's exciting to watch families who are homeless to turn their lives around," said Balk, who is also a Monroe city councilman.

Harrison said he learned about ...

Housing Hope gets financial assistance from the Bill and Melinda Gates Foundation's Sound Families Program, which funds housing and support services for homeless families in the Puget Sound region.

The county recently approved two loans — $400,000 in total — to Housing Hope to develop affordable rental housings in east county, Bolton said.

The organization has 14 affordable housing facilities in the county, including Stanwood, Marysville and Everett, but none in east county yet, Bolton said.

The Sky Valley is growing fast, and increasing housing costs are squeezing residents out of town, Balk said.

"It's difficult for existing families to find decent affordable housing," he said, adding the organization is planning to help low-income families own their homes in the area.

Homelessness has been a big issue in the valley for a long time, said Fred Walser, Sultan's police chief.

"It's not going to solve the problem, but it's a great start to solve the problem," he said.

Herald – Housing Hope starts east Snohomish County initiative (above)

Tony Balk

After a long series of meetings, they asked to become a part of Housing Hope instead of creating a new organization. In 2003, the original volunteers committed to organize an East County Branch of Housing Hope. Until this time, the agency had followed three different organizational models for community engagement and collaboration. The earliest were the Stanwood/Camano, Arlington, Lake Stevens and Marysville Action Committees. A second was the subsidiary 501(c)3 agencies that operated under Housing Hope's guidance, including Housing Hope Properties, Building Credits and the Teen Parent Housing Council. The executive director of Housing Hope also served each of these three agencies and board members were approved by Housing Hope's board. The third collaboration model was through affiliation agreements with other agencies such as the Red Cross, VOA, YWCA, Little Red Schoolhouse, Interfaith Association, Salvation Army and others.

The Housing Hope East County Branch represented a new fourth model. It planned programs in its region (defined by the boundaries of the Snohomish, Monroe, Sultan, Index and Skykomish school districts) and was responsible for fundraising, public relations and board management, but the main Housing Hope board retained both financial and fiduciary responsibilities. A regional manager position was created, thanks to funding from Impact Capital, and provision was made for the president of the branch board to serve on Housing Hope's board of directors.

These four models provided Housing Hope great flexibility of operation and produced widespread local support. Avoiding the image of a distant agency coming in and running things from the top down in a large county with 20 cities and towns, the agency was able to generate and maintain crucial citizen involvement in programs inspired by its mission and track record. Housing Hope was focused on how to get government and citizenry to collaborate. This is how federal, state and local programs succeed. Governments, which have funding to address priority social issues, want to spend money where their dollars can be multiplied and they depend on community interest and action to bring this about. Citizens want to see their tax monies well spent and effectively managed. Nonprofits succeed when they bring these two parts of the equation together to multiply resources and produce tangible results. When this happens, everyone benefits. When it doesn't, failure becomes a theme labored by demagogues hungry for power, and civil society suffers.

Early in its planning, the East Branch board adopted a goal of creating 100 affordable housing units. Veronica Haywood had previously located an available five-plex in Sultan suitable for transitional housing, and in March of 2004, Housing Hope purchased this property, later to be named Winter's Creek South, and another nearby vacant property for future development. The East Branch organized its development plan around the service-enriched housing continuum concept. When discussing priorities for development it became aware that home ownership promised one of the greatest likelihoods for quick success. Also, an important principle for development was fostering healthy community, both within the housing complexes being created as well as for the broader community.

Back in 1990, Housing Hope had investigated the St. James Apartments in Monroe as a possible site for transitional housing, but the building was dilapidated; funding was problematic, and, rather than risk failure, the agency held off expanding to the east for a decade. In the same way, the house in Edmonds was eventually abandoned and Housing Hope has yet to enter the dense urban hive in the county's southwest corner. Both efforts represented what Ed calls 'bunny trails' that ultimately lead nowhere or disappear down black holes. Starting from scratch, Housing Hope, or any similar agency, necessarily spends time and money following these in search of suitable properties and leveraging possibilities. Most end up in bunny trails, but others lead to favorable ends. The constant effort they require is a cost of doing business.

Planning for an east county program was complex. Surveys indicated that home ownership would be better received by the public than an emergency shelter. The latter tended to trigger community controversy. Many of the new east residents had moved to rural areas specifically to get AWAY from the problems emergency shelters represented. In fact, Housing Hope's Stanwood facility was the last emergency shelter it developed. The Monroe Gospel Women's Mission operated an emergency shelter for single women in Monroe, Cocoon House served youth, and YWCA was planning a small transitional housing project. Low-income housing had to be finessed: the affordability of land was an issue and infrastructure, such as public transit, was in short supply. To be effective, housing had to be located on the limited transit corridors with access to shopping and services. And because low-income housing was often perceived as problematic by rural retirees, program staff had to make sure that they were well managed.

Mark Lewinski

But images of low-income families pulling themselves up by their bootstraps and single moms donning carpenter belts to build houses for themselves and their children were likely to capture the imagination of communities, rather than threaten local residents with side issues. If their stories were well told, the more difficult affordable housing issues could be broached. Quietly, In September 2004, Winter's Creek Village North in Sultan was announced as Housing Hope's second project in the east. With huge support from Kirtley Cole and CEO Mark Lewinski, a general contracting firm who led an effort to get donated labor and materials for the construction and assistance from Master Builders Association, the work began. Two years later, just before Christmas 2006, with 11 housing units, the development received its certificate of occupancy and was quickly filled with 11 no-longer-homeless families.

Initially there was some debate over whether the East Branch would host a fund-raising Stone Soup-type dinner of its own. Several on Housing Hope's Board were concerned. Would an East Branch Stone Soup-type dinner conflict with and dilute support for Housing Hope's signature event in Everett? But the East Branch Board was given the go-ahead, and it turned out there was no cause for worry. People in the Skykomish River valley wanted an event in their own home community and the Community of Hope east dinner became a mainstay for east county generosity. By 2011 and 2012 under the leadership of Branch President Tom Fahey this event was filling the room and exceeding the fundraising goals.

The Housing Hope North Branch Board, 2004

In the northern part of the county, construction of transitional and Self Help Housing went forward with gusto. In October of 2001, the Arlington Action Committee held a fundraising dinner at the Hawthorn Inn at Smokey Point, raising over $15,000 for the Maple Leaf Meadows project, originally two long farm lots, each with a roadside house. The Arlington Action Committee raised a total of $125,000 and the Gates Foundation provided another $175,000 that Housing Hope leveraged into $2.9 million for a 22-unit development, which included 12 units of transitional housing that opened in May of 2003. In September, property was purchased in Stanwood for the Port Susan Condominiums, a new sweat equity project where ten families completed homes in 2006 and ten more in 2007.

In February of 2002 the first of Groups 17, 18, 19 and 20 began work on 32 Self Help units on a five-acre site called The Bluff in Arlington. That June, the city of Arlington celebrated Housing Hope Day, but The Bluff became one of the more star-crossed ventures in the agency's portfolio. Homebuilding is always a speculative venture, and in every project many decisions need to be made before financing is completed and funds become available. Because demand for housing in the area was high, land was more expensive than the agency would have liked. The 32 Self Help units were a huge success, meeting a significant need in Arlington. However, six lots were unsuitable for the program because of the steep slope of the land. When efforts to sell the lots were unsuccessful, the agency decided to build duplexes on each of them on speculation. Unfortunately, the duplexes proved to be unpopular locally and there were no immediate buyers. Ultimately the six units were sold, but the agency lost nearly $100,000.

Stanwood Ambassadors, 2004 (left to right) Rose Moa, Carol Jensen, Irene Amundsen, Karen Wernli, Bernice Hanson, Della Tiede

There wasn't much Housing Hope could do about the market, but The Bluff's difficulties underscored an organizational problem. The action committees had been staffed from their inception by Housing Hope's executive director, Ed, but he felt he had spread himself too thinly in the process. In 2004, the agency brought north Snohomish County representatives from the committees together to discuss the best approach for future development. If they reorganized themselves into a regional strategic development group along the lines of the East County Branch, they could better serve housing needs in the northern part of the county. Carol

Jensen and other members of her convivial Stanwood Action Committee wanted to stay together to support the Lervick Family Village program and they took the name Stanwood Housing Hope Ambassadors. The North Branch Board was organized and Carol agreed to serve both on the North Branch Board and continue work with the Ambassadors.

The North Branch served Snohomish County north of Everett in an area defined by the boundaries of the Marysville, Arlington, Stanwood/Camano, Granite Falls and Darrington school districts. Like the East County Branch, it elected a board of directors whose president served simultaneously on Housing Hope's board. The two branches developed on slightly different timetables, but by May of 2004, both had recruited representatives to serve on fundraising committees, a regional manager had been selected to support the boards, meeting space had been established, top prospects for charitable gifts had been identified, and by the end of the year, strategic plans for their regions had been created.

The Bill and Melinda Gates Foundation

In the area of giving, none could match The Bill and Melinda Gates Foundation created through the tremendous success of the Microsoft Corporation and the wealth accumulated by Bill Gates Jr. Founded in 1999 under the leadership of Bill Gates Sr., the first Executive Director, the Gates Foundation established the Sound Families Initiative in 2000. This occurred in large part out of the passionate concern by Melinda Gates over the travesty of family homelessness. In collaboration with the state of Washington, the cities of Tacoma, Seattle and Everett, and Pierce, King and Snohomish Counties, the initiative sought to triple the supply of transitional housing and services to homeless families in the three-county area over three years. It would take seven years, but the Foundation's $40 million investment leveraged public and private funds to a total of over $200 million, enabling Sound Families to create 1,460 housing units and serve 2,700 homeless children in that time. This signaled the arrival of a new philanthropic presence nationally and globally on a scale even greater than the earlier Carnegie, Ford and Rockefeller foundations, and it quickly became the largest in the world. From its founding in 1975, Microsoft had grown into a company of virtually cosmic proportion. Bill Gates Jr. regularly contended with his colleague Paul Allen and with Warren Buffett and Mexico's Carlos Slim Helu for the title of richest man in the world, and Buffett would eventually marry his immense philanthropic capacity with the Gates Foundation's.

Deanna Dawson, from County Executive Aaron Reardon's office; Bob Davis, Executive Director of HASCO; and Dave Koenig, City of Everett Planning and Community Development Manager became founding members of the Gates Foundation's Initiative's Sound Families Steering Committee, a group of 24 governmental officials, researchers and public and private agency heads, who helped guide the Initiative's progress. These three relied on Housing Hope's experience, and the agency became a leading participant in the Initiative's work. The steering committee defined and established desired outcomes, and it generated the most comprehensive analysis of family homelessness ever conducted in the state. In 2001 the Foundation contracted with the University of Washington Northwest Institute for Children and Families (NICF), a group within the UW's School of Social Work, to evaluate outcomes.

As one of the Initiative's first beneficiaries, Housing Hope received a $189,000 grant to build ten apartments, which would include units for homeless teen mothers, at New Century House. In 2003 the Gates Foundation offered the agency an unparalleled grant of $1,374,000 to develop 50 units of transitional housing at a series of planned and future facilities. The old saw says 'the man who pays the piper calls the tune,' and at a board retreat in 2003, members discussed the fateful implications of this grant. If they

TUESDAY'S Herald

SEPTEMBER 18, 2007

Health and home

Gates Foundation funds help former addict rebuild her life

Suzanne Schmid / The Herald

Kristy Geyer and her daughter, Summer Hebener, 2, watch a kids' program together in their Everett home Thursday evening. Geyer benefited from a Gates Foundation program that has provided millions of dollars for housing in Snohomish County.

By Sharon Salyer
Herald Writer

If Bill and Melinda Gates ever wonder about the impact their foundation's $9.47 million has made in the lives of homeless families in Snohomish County, they might want to listen to Kristy Geyer's story.

Her drug problems, whi- she said started at age 15, ended with addiction to methamphetamine. Eventually, she lost both her house and custody of her daughter, she said.

She spent six months at ... Manor, an Everett ... treatment ... to Pathways for Women, a program of the YWCA.

There, she said she found counseling, classes and "every resource you can possibly think of" to help her. Perhaps most importantly, this included a place to call home, a voucher to live at Family Tree Apartments in Everett.

... a steadiness ... said she has been drug-free for two years. She regained custody of her daughter, Summer Hebener, who will turn 3 in December.

Geyer, 28, has enrolled at Edmonds Community College, earning a 3.7 grade point average last quarter.

See HOME, back page, this section

Housing Hope partners with Bill & Melinda Gates Foundation

accepted the grant, they would be deeply committed to family homelessness and the essential fundraising needed to complete and sustain the Sound Families projects for years to come. Critics argued that this would mark a pivotal turning point which would limit Housing Hope's development and skew its program directions, possibly forever. In the end the board decided to accept the grant because it could be used to leverage tremendous new resources and because it was nicely aligned with Housing Hope's vision of a service-enriched housing continuum. Also, new low-income permanent housing could be developed alongside the transitional housing funded by Sound Families, thereby maintaining the agency's housing continuum balance. Housing Hope became a major local beneficiary of the Foundation's largess. The Sound Families Initiative was the most sophisticated and significant homeless family program in the region, and to the extent that the agency helped carry out this initiative in place of doing something else, the Gates Foundation did reshape Housing Hope's mission. But rather than become constrained by the Gates Foundation grant, the evaluation provided by the Sound Families project in 2007 enabled the agency to make a strategic turn in a productive new direction.

New Presidents Step Up

During this eventful time a series of thoughtful individuals presided over Housing Hope's board of directors, sharing their unique skills. The Reverend Mark Samuelson, in the background at the creation of both the NSCAC and Housing Hope, saw both agencies into the new millennium, serving nine years on the Housing Hope board and as its president from July 1998 to June 2001. It was during his tenure that Connie Niva challenged the board to take better care of its properties, and Mark had each member select a property to care for and make sure that the lawns were mowed. This was also when Todd Morrow asked how Housing Hope was going to take care of the poorest of the poor, and Samuelson guided the board in its decision to trust the community to support services rather than rely primarily on rental income. The search for a signature fundraising event was initiated. Ross Rettenmier - standout basketball player for Everett High School and Gonzaga University - and basketball fan Dr. Tom Cooper agreed to lead a community 3-on-3 basketball tournament, which the group named HoopJam. With active assistance from VISTA Volunteer Bret Leone, the tournament was held in the summers of 1997 and 1998 but results were meager.

The idea of converting Stone Soup into a fundraising dinner emerged under Mark's reign, and with future board president Jimmy Yamauchi leading the way, the new Stone Soup era began. Also during Mark's tenure, the successful $1 million Keep Hope Alive campaign was completed to solve the property upkeep challenge of the organization. Connie Niva succeeded Mark Samuelson and served as president until June 2004, energetically overseeing fundraising growth through Stone Soup and presiding at the crucial board retreat when the role of the Gates Foundation was discussed. She oversaw the implementation of Housing Hope's first series of multi-year foundation grants, the beginnings of the College of Hope, and in 2003, completed a feasibility study and launched the Build, Serve, Sustain campaign which leveraged $1.6 million in public donations and $5.3 million in contributions to obtain $29 million in grants and low-interest loans to build 270 units of housing, the largest building expansion in Housing Hope's history.

3-on-3 basketball tournament (top)
Hoop Jam shirt worn by Housing Hope volunteers (bottom)

After Connie, Fred Safstrom served two years as board president (through June, 2006) and guided Housing Hope's development of the East and North Branches. With his expertise from previous positions as president of Cascade Bank and then executive director for the development of the new Everett Events Center, Fred also helped the agency expand reserves dedicated to capital replacement, answering Connie's charge to take better care of agency properties. This was not for regular upkeep like cleaning or utilities that were paid for with rental income, but for larger investments such as putting on a new roof, acquiring appliances or upgrading wiring and plumbing. Like services, maintenance is not as 'sexy' as building something from scratch, and good stewardship and availability of a replacement fund were needed. Rather than go to the public with a tin cup every time one building or another needed a major upgrade, the solution was to have dedicated funds in place. Investing Keep Hope Alive funds wisely has provided Housing Hope an inflation-proofed principal balance, so that the buying power would remain intact.

During Fred's tenure Housing Hope also increased the amount of its SHOP funding by switching providers from HAC to Community Frameworks (CF), an agency located in Washington state with offices in Spokane and Bremerton, which provided the agency $15,000 per lot, $5,000 more than had HAC. In 2005, the agency also created the position of housing and loan counselor in order to expand its housing counseling capacity to help Self Help participants obtain loans for their houses. When the Great Recession hit in 2008 Community Frameworks helped its SHOP partner housing agencies, by forgiving one third of the $15,000 SHOP loan as soon as a new owner received the key to the house, rather than waiting ten years. Further, the forgiven funds were unrestricted as long as they were used toward affordable housing. Housing Hope was free to do what it wanted with the money, and since the organization is singularly devoted to affordable housing, it was able to use the funds to support its budget and solidify liquidity. In 2012, the SHOP revolving fund used to purchase lots for single-family sweat equity homeownership had grown to about $1 million.

Coast Real Estate, 2005- 2006

Some recall Fred's time as president, as one where the board and organization learned what NOT to do. During this tenure Housing Hope had to decide to let go of the task of property management and outsource the responsibility to an outside contractor. It was a capability the agency had built up and took pride in over the prior 17 years. Housing Hope had developed five core competencies, each of which required expertise: housing development, service delivery for homeless families, fundraising, property management and administration/finance. An internal tug of war developed between service managers, who advocated for residents, and property managers, who advocated for properties, and created an ongoing tension well known in the real estate industry. Both functions were emotion-laden, and arbitrating disputes became very time consuming. This challenged the agency's ability to manage its properties without drawing energy away from other priorities.

Another grant from Impact Capital made it possible to hire Jack Geary, who ran his own consulting business out of Bethesda, Maryland, to evaluate the property management program. His study provided templates for best practice property management, but Geary also suggested that the organization consider the "opportunity cost" of managing its own properties. His study concluded that the amount of time and money the agency expended on its four other core competencies eroded its ability to successfully manage its properties. The demands of excellence in this arena appeared to jeopardize the ability to conduct other core competencies at their optimal level. Geary also highlighted an economy of scale issue: in order to be effective according to Geary, a housing agency needed to operate around 600 units, and in 2005 Housing Hope had barely half that. The costs kept the agency from taking advantage of community and program opportunities that would have been otherwise available. The solution? Outsource property management to a specialized professional firm.

This was an unpleasant surprise since the agency had labored for 17 years to develop its property management department under the leadership of Aat, John Sevy and many other staff. The accomplishments of this effort were deeply valued and there was great fear that the needs of homeless residents could not be well understood by a private property management enterprise. Ed and Fred had many anguished discussions about the findings before presenting them to the board, but it was decided that the solution made sense and the agency put property management out to bid, an experience Ed likened to losing an arm. Ultimately, in the fall of 2005, the board chose Coast Real Estate Services to manage its properties, but what would be the fate of the 20 property managers that had worked so hard for Housing Hope? Several of these were hired by Coast Real Estate Services, but as word of layoffs spread through the small, closely knit agency, whose members regarded it as a kind of family, anxieties rose. Those not affected were called together, and Fred was brought in to explain why their jobs were OK, but the tension was palpable. Fred recalled feeling very much that he was the 'suit' brought in from on high to calm the restive proletariat and that "there was not a lot of trust or love in the room."

The Fruit of their Labor

But it worked out, and Housing Hope moved forward with the greatest expansion in its history. By 2006, 31 housing units of the planned 270 had been built, and five more projects in Sultan, Stanwood, south Everett and Monroe would add another 95. Over the next year, five more sites providing homes to 144 more families were on the drawing board. Connie Niva pointed out to reporters from The Herald that the housing was spread throughout the county so people could remain in their home communities and their children could remain in their schools. "We have never done anything this big. I think Housing Hope has proven they know how to do this. It's been amazing."

These projects included a Housing Hope Village expansion with 18 more units, including 9 homeless family apartments of transitional housing at Hope Village II and a 12,000 square foot adult learning center. At New Century Village, the final phase of construction added 14 units of transitional housing and 5 rental units to the 25 already there. Just south of Everett on Avondale Way, the agency was finishing work on the Avondale Village complex that provided 14 units of transitional housing.

In Stanwood, Groups 21 and 22 began building 20 homes at the Port Susan Condominium project, completed in December of 2006 and March of 2007, respectively. And planning went forward for five units

Avondale project completed in partnership with South Everett Mukilteo Rotary Club

Eleven unit new construction completed just before Christmas 2006 of transitional housing and 19 low-income rentals at what would be Lincoln Hill Village near the former Lincoln High School. At the Bluff, builder group 20 finished their eight houses. At Winter's Creek Village North, construction was underway on an 11-unit apartment complex.

In Monroe, Groups 23 at Sky Meadows East and 24 at Sky Meadows West worked on their 16 houses that were completed in November of 2007 and March of 2008, and a new 14-unit facility, Woods Creek Village, was planned. Additionally, plans were made for a significant expansion into southwestern Snohomish County and an urban homeownership project, but these were postponed. "We're developing five projects at once," Ed exclaimed; "we've never done anything like that".

Seven multi-family projects - Commerce Building, Beachwood, Housing Hope Village, Oakes Commons, Hope Village II, Avondale and New Century Village - were structured as LP and LLC entities managed by Housing Hope. Because the Housing Opportunity Fund was set up early in the agency's history to fund pre-development costs of new housing, and had grown steadily since Pioneer Bank's original contribution, large infusions of capital from the Build, Serve, Sustain Capital Campaign and from EQ2 loans brought it up to about $900,000. Banks made EQ2 investments to satisfy federal Community Reinvestment Act (CRA) requirements, but having made them, they sometimes expected a share in the agency's business. Wells Fargo Bank had made two loans to the HOF totaling $450,000 at 2% interest, which greatly contributed to housing development success. But when a deeper deposit and borrowing relationship wasn't realized with Housing Hope, they required repayment of the loans. What a bank giveth, it also may taketh away, to use in more advantageous ways for the bank. Yet in spite of these occasional setbacks, HOF and SHOP monies made it possible for the agency to take advantage of the big housing development opportunities which were critical to its success.

Expanding Tomorrow's Hope

As the number of people Housing Hope served grew, so did the number of their children, and so did Tomorrow's Hope. When it moved to the first floor of Housing Hope's new office, in 1997, it expanded from a day care into a childcare center where 40 children from Housing Hope and partner agency families in emergency and transitional housing could receive nutritious meals, health checks and education. Partners, including VOA, YWCA, the Everett Gospel Mission and the Interfaith Association of Snohomish County (the descendant of the NSCAC) valued this service for their residents. It became obvious that more space was needed, and how to accomplish this was the topic of conversations by staffers while lunching at the Peking Duck Restaurant, a popular establishment immediately south of Housing Hope's offices.

One day in 2000, they were surprised to see a For Sale sign in the restaurant's window. Obtaining this property would satisfy Tomorrow's Hope's space and parking needs. Housing Hope turned to the community for help. Donations, foundation grants, public funding and a Step Loan (a step loan's rate of interest steps up and down over time with market-rate interest) from SeaFirst Bank enabled Housing Hope

Tomorrow's Hope Child Care entrance

Ken Schilaty Family Learning Center

to buy the property and gut its interior just in time to host the first Stone Soup Dinner designed to raise funds in 2001.

With rafters and studs exposed, stories of Housing Hope's success and plans for expanded childcare made the evening a stunning success. The next day Gaffney Construction began its building renovation and four months later, Tomorrow's Hope Childcare Center opened not as a day care but as a well-equipped licensed childcare facility guided by lead teachers and assistants with expanded nutrition and transportation programs, a health clinic, and with space for 91 children, four months to five years of age.

The Peking Duck had originally been developed as a Sizzler Restaurant by developer Ken Schilaty. Ken and his family would become huge fans of Housing Hope, but this took some time. Immediately east of the restaurant building was another plot of vacant land still owned by Ken, together with his son John. The land parcel had three duplexes on an upper shelf of land facing Fleming Street to the west, leaving a vacant parcel between the restaurant and the duplexes. Since the only access to the vacant land was through Housing Hope's property, Ken arranged a meeting to discuss sale of the land and duplex property to the agency. An experienced negotiator, he had a high price in mind, but after Ed had impressed Ken with Housing Hope's work, he agreed to a price far below what he intended. Later a generous donation from Ken and his wife, Flo, resulted in naming the new facility the Schilaty Family Learning Center. Of the twelve apartments built on the site in 2004, nine were reserved for homeless families. The 3,000-square-foot family learning center became the new home of the College of Hope and also provided space for a new before- and after-school program for 21 additional children aged six through twelve.

In its new space Tomorrow's Hope continued its evolution. In 2003 the agency had participated in "One Childhood Lasts a Lifetime," a study funded by the Medina Foundation, that revealed the lack of services available to homeless children, particularly those from birth to age five, many of whom needed speech therapy and had unmet medical and health needs. In response Housing Hope created the position of child specialist to provide support and needed services at several Housing Hope sites. The child specialist made frequent in-home visits to gauge each family's needs, and taught parents how to build their children's self esteem. For many families this was the first time they had ever received such help.

Steadily, Tomorrow's Hope Childcare Center transformed into a Child Development Center where children could acquire social, emotional, physical and cognitive skills appropriate to their age. By 2008, it employed a part time child psychologist to help the child specialist provide developmental assessments and together with parents, case managers and staff, create tailored intervention plans to help children catch up in their development.

Ed's Sabbatical

In the midst of all this, Ed decided he needed a break. Board presidents came and went, but Ed had been a constant presence for all things Housing Hope. In the larger community he was described as a man who got things done. The agency attracted intelligent, committed and hard working people, but all stridently affirm Ed's extraordinary leadership and organizing skills. When he protests, they enjoy trotting out the

The Bruce and Fred Story

In 25 years, only two individuals have served both on the board of directors and as staff.

Bruce Eklund and Fred Safstrom

Bruce Eklund was a founder of Housing Hope in 1987 and served one year on the board to help get the organization launched. Over the years, Bruce's family adopted and supported one of Housing Hope's apartments and Bruce volunteered on the Services Committee of the organization. In 2006, Bruce was recruited by the Nominating Committee to a three-year term on the board, but a year into this term Ed talked Bruce into joining the staff as the chief operating officer, where he served for four years.

Fred Safstrom became a nine-year board member emeritus in 2006. He was elected to the board of directors in 1997, serving as treasurer and later as president from 2004 to 2006. In 2007, upon the retirement of John Sevy as housing director, Fred was recruited to fill a temporary housing developer position. Fred's depth of organizational understanding and his accomplished performance quickly led to promotion to housing director. In 2009, a new deputy executive director position was created to free Ed up for strategic initiatives, and Fred was promoted into this significant leadership role.

story of the sabbatical he took from mid-January to mid-April of 2004 to catch his breath physically and mentally after working full-bore in the trenches for 17 years. But his idea of a restorative sabbatical was very much his and Carol's own. They flew down to sunny, tropical Belize where, Peace Corps to the bone, they volunteered with Habitat For Humanity to set up an affiliate in the southern part of the country and gathered committed people to serve on a new board Ed had formed that ultimately built nine houses during the three months they were there. And when the Petersen children and grandchildren visited during their busy rest, the reassembled family energetically scaled Mayan pyramids and snorkeled the coastal keys.

An ulterior reason for his 'break' was to see if the agency could stand on its own. As soon as he left, however, board members felt the vacuum of leadership and were unsure how to proceed. It did not quite devolve to screeching chimpanzees swinging from draperies with lampshades on their heads, but all were vastly relieved when he showed up tanned, relaxed and raring to go. In his absence, plans for the agency's involvement in the Monte Cristo Hotel went awry and, to his perplexity, slipped away. The question of what would happen if Ed were struck by lightning or hit by a bus became a growing concern.

After Fred, Ken Nelson - whose wife, Carol, was now CEO of Cascade Bank - became board President from 2006 to 2007. During Ken's tenure Housing Hope continued growing the HOF and finished capitalizing its Service Sustaining Fund. The Fortune Family Foundation had a strong presence during these years. In 2005 it provided $15,000 for Housing Hope to hire a videographer, Legacy Productions, to develop an informational video for the agency to use with its speakers' bureau and in fundraising. Building on this, in July of 2007, the Foundation provided a $200,000 challenge grant to double Housing Hope's fundraising capacity over three years, from $400,000 annually to $800,000, by searching out and cultivating donors and converting them into annual givers. To encourage maximum effort during the first year, the Foundation offered Housing Hope $50,000 once it had raised $550,000, to reach the $600,000 goal. Once this heavy lifting was done and it had raised $625,000 the next year, the Foundation would give $75,000, to raise the total to $700,000, and another $75,000 the third year after it had raised $725,000, thus achieving the goal of $800,000. And so it happened.

Another significant development happened in this period. For the first time Housing Hope dipped into its pool of talented board volunteers to enhance its staffing. Founding board member Bruce Eklund and former board president Fred Safstrom joined the staff, providing grounded leadership and continuity of passion for the Housing Hope mission.

Chapter 6 Into The Great Recession: 2007-2012

In December of 2007 the agency purchased 35 lots in Stanwood for a Self Help Housing building site it would call Copper Station. It would be the last land purchase Housing Hope made for several years as the economy collapsed. The Global Financial Crisis began when housing prices in the United States collapsed toward the end of 2007.

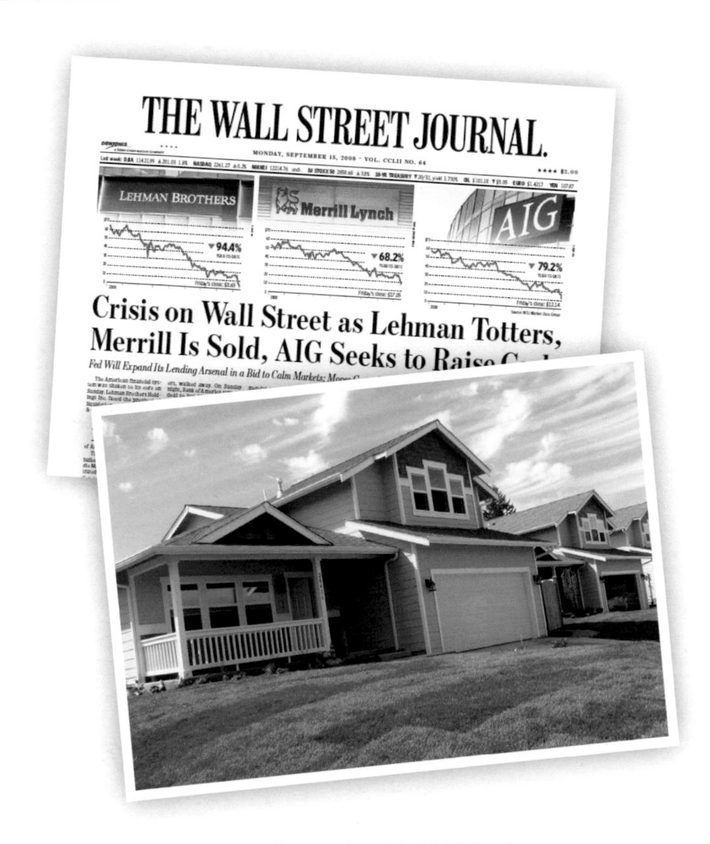
THE WALL STREET JOURNAL.

Crisis on Wall Street as Lehman Totters,
Merrill Is Sold, AIG Seeks to

The Wall Street Journal, September 15, 2008 (top)
One of 35 Self Help houses constructed at Copper Station (bottom)

Low interest rates and an influx of foreign capital during previous years had led to a boom in housing construction, fueled by optimistic buyers who had taken out sub-prime or risky loans to buy more house than they could afford. Locally, the rise in housing prices beginning in the '70s and of homelessness in the '80s and '90s were a result of this trend. Increasingly, homeowners saw their houses less as places to live than as investments to be sold later for profit. Second and third mortgages were taken out to finance affluent life styles, encouraged by bankers who argued that increasing housing prices guaranteed future sellers the ability to pay down their increasing debt load. Government encouraged deregulation to spur business, and as the housing boom became a bubble, banks worldwide invested in U.S. housing to maximize their profits. By mid-2007, however, a rise in interest rates meant loans went into default and foreclosures became more common. But this was only a symptom of a deeper malaise.

In much the same way as homeowners collateralized their homes to fund affluent life styles, investment bankers and hedge fund managers used clever financial instruments such as derivatives—contracts between partners based on the assumption of the future value of securities (something financially valuable) — to generate enormous profits for themselves and their participating lenders. As long as these derivatives found buyers, everyone seemed to win. But this system, based on imaginary value, turned out to be a house of cards.

When Lehman Brothers, the fourth largest investment bank in the United States, filed for bankruptcy on September 15, 2008, the country entered what become known as the Great Recession. Three days later Treasury Secretary Henry Paulson and Federal Reserve Chairman Ben Bernanke met with congressional leaders to propose an immense federal bailout of collapsing financial institutions, and Bernanke told them, "If we don't do this, we may not have an economy on Monday". The sharp drop in housing prices from their peak in 2006 caused home equity to drop by trillions of dollars. Also losing trillions were retirement funds, savings and investment assets, and the value of securities which were backed by mortgages. By the time Wall Street's Dow Jones Industrial Average had plummeted 52% from a high of nearly 14,000 in October of 2007 to 6,626 by March of 2009, the nation was estimated to have lost a quarter of its wealth.

Among the host of financial institutions that failed or were taken over by the government, the poster child in Washington State was Washington Mutual Bank, the largest savings and loan association in the country. Its collapse in 2008 was the largest bank failure in American history. "We were petrified," recalls Ed Petersen, "when we learned that WAMU was in trouble." As housing prices plummeted and foreclosures spiked, credit froze and housing construction stopped. With that, low-income housing tax credits for the construction of affordable housing had no value. The deals Housing Hope leveraged that required these tax credits were no longer viable. No new projects could be financed through this source.

The bankruptcy of WAMU and its subsequent purchase by JPMorgan Chase & Co. highlighted a profound change in banking practice as local banks were bought out and absorbed by larger national banks. When local banks that had cultivated relationships with communities for generations became subsumed into larger institutions whose headquarters and interests were elsewhere, a vital economic relationship was lost. People involved in Housing Hope's finances bemoan the disappearance of these devoted contacts that were so crucial to its success. In 1993 WAMU had bought out Pioneer Bank; in 2010 Frontier Bank was seized by regulators, and sold to Union Bank of California. And in 2011, Cascade Bank was bought out by Opus Bank of California. Fortunately, in WAMU's case, JPMorgan Chase also had an interest in local economic empowerment, and in 2009 the JP Morgan Chase Foundation provided a $40,000 grant to help the agency finish the Woods Creek project in Monroe. Everett general contractor Kirtley Cole Associates helped organize other local contractors and vendors to donate labor and materials for Winter's Creek North in Sultan. This assistance underscored the value of local relationships, and the Master Builders Care Foundation awarded its Golden Nugget award to Kirtley Cole for this generosity and skillful leadership.

Windermere Passion

The collapse of the housing bubble and of so many financial institutions starved the national economy, and surviving businesses tightened their belts. The resulting nosedive in business and corporate giving can be measured in the amounts raised at the Snohomish County Windermere Foundation golf tournaments. Starting in 1995, the foundation organized an annual golf tournament with all proceeds dedicated to Housing Hope. In the early years these events generated $30,000 annually to support Housing Hope programs. However, from 2008 the economy took a huge bite out of the tournament with results reduced to $15,000 or less. And this was possible only by resorting to bizarre gimmicks like selling mulligans—chances to redo a bad shot—or by selling ropes of licorice to reach from where a ball landed to the hole. All of this tortured Doug Adams from Windermere's Alderwood office, a golfer who loved

Doug Adams - Windermere Golf Tournament Chair for 18 years

the game and had managed the tournaments since their inception. Until the state cracked down on the practice, one could get title companies to sponsor holes, and WAMU would kick in $10,000 as an event sponsor. Now the foundation struggled to get sponsors. But as it always had, in good times and bad, the community stepped up and gave. Housing Hope has always put its trust in the community, and the community has always responded generously. And Union Bank, which in 2010 bought out Frontier Bank, where Tim Otani landed after the WAMU closure, stepped up to sponsor the Windermere Foundation golf tournaments in 2011 and 2012. At the time of this writing, results once again exceed $15,000, and optimism for the future has returned.

Ideas for Consideration

With the onset of hard times, Housing Hope had to consider new ways of carrying out its mission. When Kathleen Horner became board president after Ken Nelson in July of 2008, she brought with her planning and marketing skills refined as the head of Stockpot, Inc, a division of the Campbell Soup Company. As a significant employer, she had asked Everett officials how she might establish strong relationships with community groups, and they suggested Housing Hope and in particular fundraising for Stone Soup. When she provided the soup for the dinner and hosted it in 2004, the nominating committee asked her to join the board. There she focused on the budget and noted that the agency struggled to accurately predict its fundraising potential, so she pushed for more sophisticated use of numbers to measure revenue streams in order to develop better strategic plans. But she also looked at the organization itself and initiated a probing critique of its internal dynamic.

Kathleen had the board agree to a more rigorous approach to strategic planning by adopting an annual rolling three-year process with objectives that could be measured. Such a plan would pose and answer key strategic questions: what did the board see happening in those years? What three or four related issues keep members up at night, and how should these be addressed? She urged the use of SWOT analysis and that the board be apprised quarterly of progress and problems encountered implementing the plan.

SWOT document

A crucial element in budgeting and planning was marketing, her forte, and she conducted a workshop for the board on building a strategic marketing plan that mirrored the more general strategic plan. The agency needed to look at itself and ask: if donors have a choice, why would they give to Housing Hope? To keep donors committed, what did the agency need to deliver in a three year period? And how would it identify and measure its success? The ability to do this could let the agency know how much money it had to raise and how it could best present programs to donor audiences. And who were these audiences? The board needed to analyze the donor base in order to help the agency tailor its fundraising activities. If, for example, the most significant group of donors were boomers, then font size should be enhanced to ensure that they could be read without difficulty. If a significant number were retirees, these folks had more time to be interested and focused than 20- or 30-year-olds and each required different approaches. In a changing social and economic environment, donors were shifting loyalties from multiple recipients to prioritizing two or three charities with agendas where a donor believed they could make a greater difference. New donors tended to be better educated, well-traveled, and more likely to select projects they could believe in. But to know how to best relate to them the agency needed to collect demographic and donor data.

Michael Dotson, Bank of America VP surprises Housing Hope with a $200,000 Neighbor Builder grant announcement

Kathleen refocused attention on the idea that Housing Hope represented a brand, and that developing brand identity was a way to invite supporters to understand what Housing Hope really represented. She observed that...

Housing Hope had, in her words, "cracked the code" of homelessness; that it had found a way to help homeless people deal with their situation more successfully than had any other agency.

Its challenge now was to better tell its story to the right audience. Housing Hope provided homes, helped people assess their strengths and weaknesses and helped them find and keep jobs. It helped mothers learn child-raising skills and how to budget time and money effectively. It helped educate children and helped families enter the housing market. Housing Hope provided all of these benefits, and provided residents the experience of success. A lot of agencies did one or a few of these things, but no one had put it all together in the way Housing Hope had. It had cracked the code, and stories about how it succeeded in doing this were its primary marketing resource.

Though times were hard, Kathleen and others were optimistic enough to think that the agency could use these times as an opportunity to look at Housing Hope's internal culture and enhance its resiliency and flexibility to more effectively move forward. She also challenged the board to consider what would happen if Ed "got run over by a bus". A stronger leadership development plan and succession plan was needed.

New Roles

While Kathleen was taking a hard look at Housing Hope's internal culture, Ed was reconsidering his role. By this time Housing Hope had learned how to do what it did well, and tweaking this program or that was not as energizing or as much fun for him as had been building an agency out of whole cloth. He went to the board and told them he needed to change his job to focus on one of the most daunting challenges facing the agency. Stable housing, even with supportive services, did not make families self sufficient: the question was how their incomes could be increased.

A distressing conclusion drawn from the Gates Sound Families Initiatives was that overall improvements in housing, education and job training enabled homeless families in King, Pierce and Snohomish Counties to increase their average hourly pay about 20% from $9 to $11, but jobs paying $20 an hour were needed for them to obtain permanent housing on their own without any additional subsidy. And given a great and prolonged recession, not to mention the historic shift from high-paying manufacturing jobs to lower-paying service jobs, those jobs were largely unavailable. One could build the housing units, provide day care, counseling, job training, even enable low-income people to build their own homes, but, ultimately, if there were not jobs available paying a genuine living wage, which was far more than the mandated minimum wage, the specter of homelessness would continue to bedevil the community.

Housing Hope had control of a key product line: it owned its own housing, provided its own child care and taught clients job and life skills. It did not depend on any other agency to do this, but it had no control over providing the jobs that could ensure a client's self-sufficiency. It did not have the ability to increase wages. How could it help families earn higher wages? What would it take to put people on career paths and educate them to get the credentials and skills necessary for economic independence? These were questions that intrigued Ed, and he wanted to find the answers. More to the point, he wanted Housing Hope to develop a program that would do this.

In 2010, at the annual strategic planning retreat, the board took a hard, long look at his proposal. Was the agency ready to launch something of this magnitude? Would it put Housing Hope's reputation and bank account at risk? And would any board members volunteer to help put such a program together? Four raised their hands: Laura Brent, Kathy Burgoyne, Paul Vexler and Bill Yoakum. HopeWorks, a runner-up name in the 1987 selection process to name the agency, reappeared and was selected as the name of a new nonprofit employment agency. It would spawn a series of remarkable new initiatives.

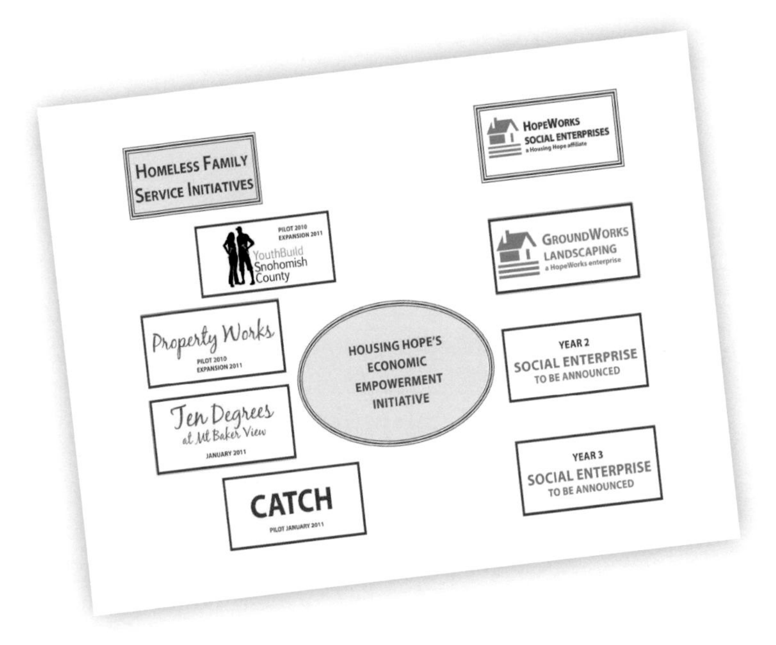

Chart depicting new employment initiative

Making Hope Work: The Economic Empowerment Initiative

HopeWorks capitalized on what the agency had already accomplished. Here a summative background for the HopeWorks initiative will provide the framework for this innovative and ambitious new development plan. The idea for such a program had been around since Housing Hope's beginning, when it was well understood that people were homeless due to the high cost of housing and for a variety of other reasons, chief among them trouble in dealing with what life threw at them. Leo Tolstoy opens Anna Karenina with the line "All happy families are alike; all unhappy families differ in their own way." Whether caused specifically by lack of job skills, a violent environment, drug use, mental problems or a host of other disabilities, their differing forms of unhappiness - moving in with others, couch surfing, living in cars or on the street - resulted from not knowing how to handle overwhelming circumstances. Many of the deficiencies were in life skills: how to communicate, how to balance a checkbook, how to show up on time for work day after day, how to learn and how to work hard. Historically, social critics have branded this effort as turning people into middle class bourgeoisie; indeed these are the hallmarks of middle-class morality, as Alfred P. Doolittle, Eliza's father in My Fair Lady had sniffed, but the point was to give these homeless families the skills necessary to become middle class if they chose to do so. And because every unhappy family or individual was different in its own unhappy way, each had to be approached individually. That is why every program that sought this end proved difficult to manage and expensive to operate. Could it even be done?

Caseworkers dealt with life skills but often did not have the time and the full fund of knowledge in all necessary skill areas. Moreover, even though Housing Hope had become aware very early on that life skill deficits existed and that these skills needed to be taught, it was too busy meeting other more immediate priorities to develop a model to meet this need. In earlier years Housing Hope had help to do so. Working with the Private Industry Council and Community Trades and Careers to complete employment assessments, the agency hired staff to provide guidance in parenting skills, to assess clients' hirable skills, and help with education and job training. Case managers provided some well-child training; teachers and staff counseled parents with children in Tomorrow's Hope, and nurses provided pregnant women and teen mothers with pre-natal and child care information, but these were add-ons and did not constitute comprehensive programs.

By the late 1990s Housing Hope, in collaboration with partner agencies, had accumulated enough experience to determine that the skills homeless families typically lacked fell into four categories: economic well-being, health and wellness, family life and housing expertise. In 1999 Housing Hope convened a meeting with four agencies: Deaconess Children's Service, the Community Health Center, Operation Improvement and Housing Hope to devise a model that drew upon each organization's competency in order to support a coordinated life skills program. Deaconess focused on family life; the Community Health Center on health and wellness; Operation Improvement on economic well-being; and Housing Hope on housing expertise. An Innovation Grant of $10,000 from United Way allowed the four to put together a demonstration project whose pilot would be located at Beachwood Apartments in Marysville. Originally called the Partners Opportunity Project, it would eventually be named The College of Hope.

The College of Hope: A Key Building Block

Originally Todd Morrow and Connie Niva didn't like the name College of Hope because it sounded too lofty. Ed, however, liked it specifically because it was lofty, and he thought it communicated high expectations for the program's participants. When College of Hope was chosen, Todd and Connie teasingly asked why their opinion was asked in the first place, but Ed just smiled his beatific smile, musing perhaps that they should consider themselves lucky that he did not invite them out for lunch, as Barbara Lamoureux would have warned them.

Many contributed to the success of this effort, but one of the more significant was a Beachwood resident we will call Karina. Having moved to Marysville with her family from Canada when she was eight, she went to a series of Christian schools and graduated from Watson Groen Christian School in Seattle and Shoreline Christian High School. She had worked since she was 13, first delivering newspapers, then as an aide in a nursing home and later as a restaurant cook. She went to beauty school, earned a certificate as a cosmetologist and got married. Then things fell apart. When her son was only an infant, she had to flee from her husband, due to domestic violence and his abuse of drugs and alcohol. Her sister helped get her into an Everett shelter on Hewitt Avenue. Through the YWCA Pathways for Women program she connected with Housing Hope and, working as a teacher's aide and lead teacher, she qualified for a low-income apartment at Beachwood where she lived for more than four years. Shortly after moving into the Beachwood Apartments, Karina became romantically involved with a really good man. After finding out she was pregnant, they made plans to get married, but tragically - he died suddenly when she was only ten weeks along. With no child support and another on the way, she continued working as a pre-school teacher until her daughter was born, at which time she applied for a three bedroom apartment and enrolled her children in Tomorrow's Hope. After proving paternity, she was able to collect social security for her daughter which enabled her to stay at home to take care of her children for the next two years.

During this time Karina became more involved with the Beachwood community and was hired to be its 'key holder', the after-hours contact person who handled emergencies, and she became a member of the Beachwood community resident council. When the demonstration pilot program for the College of Hope was organized at Beachwood, she became its on-site advocate and worked with VISTA to develop the program and get residents involved. After the first year she was asked to sign up for a second year as a VISTA volunteer and continued to build the program, developing its childcare program, transportation options, and relations with other community service providers. In the summer of 2002 Karina was hired to fill the first staff position at the College of Hope and for the next six years she developed its data tracking system and coordinated all events and classes. In the summer of 2002, she applied for and was hired to be College of Hope's coordinator, entering data into the program's computer systems and coordinating evening events and classes.

While living at Beachwood she became interested in the Self Help homeownership program, but wondered how anyone could devote the enormous amount of time and effort it required and still raise children. But when she heard that the agency was looking for interested families to join the program at The Bluff in Arlington she swallowed her fear and spent every weekend for the next 55 weeks building eight houses with seven other households. She often took her children with her so they could watch their own bedrooms take shape. Over time, Karina would become a successful and respected businesswoman, which makes her a sterling example of how Housing Hope helps people succeed beyond what they dared hope or imagine at the time. The Bluff proved challenging and may have been a money-pit for the agency, but for Karina and the others who built their homes there, it was pure gold.

Karina's intelligence, motivation and practical understanding got the College of Hope pilot program at Beachwood off the ground. In no small part because of her good work, the program prospered.

From Preschool to Year 13: A new Education Paradigm

Gradually, as its partner agencies altered their focus, Housing Hope assumed full responsibility for the College of Hope, and in 2004 the program moved into the newly constructed Schilaty Family Learning Center at Hope Village. Grants from Washington Mutual, Murdock Trust, Gates Foundation and Paul Allen Foundation provided for the construction of the 3,000-square-foot adult learning center. Two years later the board expanded the College of Hope program into a community-wide program providing life skills for residents of ten agencies operating affordable housing in the county. A curriculum of 37 courses ranging from pre-natal care and personal health to effective communication, parenting, group dynamics, budgeting, money management, anger management, finance, record keeping, homeownership, strategic planning and specific job skills was developed, each addressing one of the original four competencies. Classes were offered in the north, east and central areas of the county at Smokey Point, Stanwood, Monroe and Lynnwood four evenings a week.

In the process Housing Hope created a paradigm shift into a Year 13 educational model. The idea was to embed healthy attitudes toward education in all parts of the agency. Increasingly the focus became the creation of education pathways for homeless families. These were designed to serve a wide range of ages, from pre-schoolers getting ready for kindergarten to college entry for adults. This model included everyone, even those who thought college was out of reach. The Year 13 organizing philosophy was crafted as follows: "Once stable housing is provided, the next most important agenda is to help families embrace education as the pathway to a better future." The program started by helping each parent create a family development plan. For adults, it fostered education in three ways.

Proud College of Hope participants with course completion certificates (top)
Student in nutrition class (bottom)

The first was to create effective learning communities at each residential site, where participants learn from each other and take classes, and workshops are offered. Second, it developed the College of Hope and made its courses widely and conveniently available. Finally, caseworkers kept track of clients' progress, provided counsel, applauded learning accomplishments and helped them set and meet goals.

But how could you get someone who had a lousy experience in school to embrace education as the best pathway to a better future? To do this, the College of Hope employed an adult learning model termed andragogy. The traditional pedagogical model, which was likened to 'a sage on a stage,' features a teacher in front of the class telling students what to learn. Andragogy calls upon students to reflect on their everyday life experiences, which becomes the method of gaining insight for managing money, marriage, stress and self-awareness. Experiences, both success and failure, can be viewed as building blocks for future achievements: knowing what to do and what not to do. Learning how to do these things was no different than mastering the five-paragraph expository essay or algebra equation, and involved the same skills. Learning to overcome misapprehension and learn from experience is the heart of this approach.

Did it work? Clients' exit interviews indicated that for most it did. "The support and caring from the program without judgment (made a big difference). They offered us resources and did so with open arms. They had so many neat programs to help you get through that time and focus." "(The program) helped me believe in myself—that I can fix my problems." "They did a pretty good job of getting people started down the right path, like with credit counseling." Some found it difficult: "It's hard to handle a case manager coming every week. It wasn't the greatest coming to community meetings and sign up for things." Those having the most difficulty were often those who had experienced the least success in their lives, and those who had dropped out of high school were especially vulnerable and needed a different approach.

Year 13 Programs: Youth Build, PropertyWorks, Ten Degrees and CATCH

By 2012, as efforts continued to build this Year 13 model, increasing numbers of Housing Hope residents were participating in college classes. New programs were being conceived by HopeWorks, building on the education platform provided through the College of Hope. YouthBuild was the first of several special projects incubated by HopeWorks.

Housing Hope took an interest in high school dropouts when it learned that the YouthBuild program was a good fit with the agency's sweat equity construction program. Youth could learn construction skills, complete their high school equivalency diploma through Everett Community College (ECC), and earn college credits in construction through Edmonds Community College (EdCC). Housing Hope, in partnership with the federal Department of Labor, Workforce Development Council (the new name for the Private Industry Council), Everett Community College and Edmonds Community College launched YouthBuild in July, 2009. This was a ten-month program in which low-income high school dropouts over 18 years old spent 30 hours a week, divided equally between education and learning construction skills at Housing Hope's Self Help Housing sites, for which they earned at least minimum wage while building. "This program is such a boon for Snohomish County," said Sue Ambler, CEO of the Council. "Not only does it provide for academic and on-the-job occupational skills training, but it provides meaningful work for at-risk youth." Besides providing credentials the students needed to become more employable, this program also gave them an opportunity to earn college credits applied toward an associate or bachelor's degree. By June of 2010, 11 of the program's original 30+ participants walked in the Everett Community College graduation ceremony in

Youth Build participants learning construction skills and studying for GEDs

Mt. Baker View 21 unit apartment building (above)
PropertyWorks intern (left)

cap and gown to receive their GEDs, followed by 11 in 2011 and 18 in 2012. Getting a GED is an important accomplishment, but only one step on the path toward economic self-sufficiency. To expand on this "Year 13" concept, Housing Hope created another program that provided saleable skills in a line of work that it was intimately familiar with and one that could offer jobs with wage progression opportunities in the local market: property management.

In February, 2010, in partnership with Everett Community College (ECC) and Coast Real Estate, Housing Hope launched PropertyWorks, a six-month program in which students combined 20 hours of college classes in property management with 20 hours of internship working at Coast Real Estate or other property management firms to earn a Property Management Certificate qualifying them to enter the profession. Having no dedicated funding, the program was put together with considerable creativity. Classes were taught at the college by certified staff from Coast Real Estate in conjunction with ECC. Two other Everett property management firms, Quantum Management Services and Legacy Management Group, participated in providing internships. The inclusion of classes stressing sustainability and environmental practices enabled the Washington State Department of Health and Human Services to provide financing which allowed the program to provide special certificates in green maintenance and office leasing. Coast Real Estate was interested in training interns it could hire, and 9 of the first 13 interns had jobs before they completed the program. The success of this program helped the agency visualize the direction it wanted to go toward developing a program devoted to job creation. For those who wished to go further academically, Housing Hope came up with another program.

Ten Degrees was an innovative new program established in October of 2010 at the newly refurbished Mt. Baker View in Everett, the first multi-unit low-income family facility the agency developed after the housing crash of 2008. For this program Housing Hope constructed an on-site adult learning center and dedicated 10 of the 21 affordable apartments to low-income families with a head of household motivated and able to pursue an academic degree as the pathway for a better future. A children's room was included in the learning center, and families organized a daycare to tend each other's children while students worked in study groups. Housing Hope provided an on-site educational specialist to help residents learn computer and study skills, get financial aid and learn how to navigate the complexities of post-secondary education.

In February of 2011, CATCH (Creating Access To Careers in Healthcare) was launched in partnership with Edmonds Community College. A five-year federal grant provided money for training in healthcare fields, which were experiencing a shortage of trained personnel in the Puget Sound market. Housing Hope served as gatekeeper for the homeless participants, providing pathways for its residents into healthcare careers. As of spring 2012, twenty-two homeless individuals have been enrolled.

A report to the board in July 2012 indicated that 65 Housing Hope residents had participated in college classes the prior year and 29 had earned a certificate or degree. "This represents a dramatic increase over past years.

HopeWorks Social Enterprises

HopeWorks was a novel concept. Rather than provide job development and placement in the private sector, the prevalent employment agency model, a new approach would be launched. HopeWorks was created as an incubator. Its purpose was to engineer career pathways specifically for homeless households. This included several projects focused on job readiness developed within Housing Hope and a whole new approach through HopeWorks itself, in the form of new social enterprise businesses providing training and jobs designed to offer career pathways for income progression over time.

HopeWorks Board of Directors at their standard board meeting location: (L to R) Bill Yoakum, Kathy Burgoyne, Laura Brent, Paul Vexler, Leah Schedin and Bob Dent

PropertyWorks served as a demonstration project, testing Ed's idea for a new employment initiative which finally came to fruition in July 2010 when Housing Hope's board of directors adopted an Economic Empowerment Initiative, including a job readiness program. The plan called for expanding a single employment specialist position to three positions, and creating a new nonprofit, HopeWorks Social Enterprises, that would develop three new social enterprises in 2011, 2012 and 2013. To the four Housing Hope board members who had raised their hands for the HopeWorks board was added a fifth, Robert K. Dent, son of the founder of Tyee Aircraft, who was an early supporter of Housing Hope during its infancy. The R.K. Dent Transitional Housing Building at Housing Hope Village is named in honor of his support. The Boeing Company granted $50,000 to fund an enterprise developer position, filled by Mary Jonasen, and grants helped outfit and start up the first social enterprise business.

Desiring a big media splash, the agency delayed announcing the new project until January 6, 2011, when it hosted a community event in Mt. Baker View's beautiful new learning center. Sixty guests were seated along three sides of the room while in the center, the five founding members of HopeWorks' board conducted their founding meeting, electing Bill Yoakum its president, Bob Dent vice president and Laura Brent secretary, adopting by-laws and establishing the first of its social enterprises, GroundWorks Landscaping.

GroundWorks Landscaping

$15,000 in start-up money from the Fortune Family Foundation and $40,000 from Chase Bank enabled HopeWorks to purchase a truck, trailer, a fleet of lawnmowers and provide starting salaries for its employees. Signature Landscaping Services, under the leadership of CEO Mark Henning and several of his staff, provided business mentoring to help GroundWorks develop a business model and best practices. Mark had started his landscaping business out of a wheelbarrow and a set of gardening tools 30 years prior. He knew intimately the elements of starting a new enterprise of this type and he inspired confidence in what it could become. Coast Real Estate also believed in landscaping as a potential career pathway. It was Ceedee Felton, portfolio manager

The Boeing Connections

The Boeing name has gained global significance. Snohomish County is lucky to have the biggest building in the world occupied by a company that cares about its community.

The presence of Boeing seems to be everywhere and that's partly because there are three entities which each make a big splash where Housing Hope lives and works. The Boeing Corporation, Employees Combined Fund of Boeing and Boeing Employees Credit Union are distinct entities. Each has contributed mightily to the Housing Hope success over the past two decades.

The Boeing Corporation has been actively supporting Housing Hope's mission since the early 1990s. Capital grants for new housing developments, startup funding for new projects, operating support, in-kind printing and items from the Boeing surplus warehouse have all helped build the agency's success. In 2005 an agreement was reached to recruit a Boeing representative to be elected to the Housing Hope board and serve as liaison between the company and the nonprofit. Bill Yoakum, Director for Production Engineering has served in this capacity and in 2011 became the President of HopeWorks Social Enterprises, the new employment agency created by Housing Hope. And Robert Walker who heads an engineering group at Boeing also serves on the Housing Hope Board.

The Employees Community Fund of Boeing raises funds from 80,000 employees who work for Boeing in the Puget Sound region. They distribute grants to community agencies and programs after reviewing community needs, setting criteria and evaluating applications. Trustees visit each eligible program to learn first hand about the proposed project. Housing Hope has been the beneficiary of nineteen ECF grants totaling $445,320, which have paid for a childcare van, playground, a roof for Crossroads Shelter, appliances, capital acquisitions and improvements.

Boeing Employees Credit Union (BECU) was created to serve employees of the company but today serves employees and the community at large. In recent years, rapid growth of the company has created a dramatic presence in Snohomish County and an increasing ability to provide charitable support to affordable housing and other priority needs. Vikki Strand represents BECU on the Housing Hope board. In 2012 a three year pledge of operating support for the new economic empowerment initiative of the agency is resulting in a deeper and more powerful alliance.

for Coast in collaboration with Karen Matson, Social Service Director for Housing Hope who originally conceived the idea of a landscaping program to employ Housing Hope residents. At Housing Hope's behest, Coast Real Estate provided the first contracts for landscaping services at Housing Hope's 18 multifamily properties.

The second enterprise is called WaterWorks Irrigation Services with operations initiated in late spring 2012. The third social enterprise will roll out in 2013. As of the writing of this book it has yet to be announced, but it will surely reflect the collaboration—synergy is the hot term—and planning of all the parts of Housing Hope working together to find new ways to fulfill its mission.

It took Housing Hope ten years to go from startup to establish Housing Hope Village as a home for the organization and it was 17 years before the 4 acre campus was complete. The power of this centralized and comprehensive location for Housing Hope's mission has provided the inspiration to imagine a home called HopeWorks Station for the new employment initiative. This development is envisioned to encompass a city block with seven to ten social enterprises, a training academy, 100 or more housing units and a headquarters for HopeWorks to oversee its mission. As with Housing Hope, the idea was for HopeWorks to control its own product line: social enterprise businesses that supplied internships, jobs and referrals to aligned employers. Time will tell how far this vision will be realized but there's no doubt that the organization's "can do" attitude will be in full play.

The first five HopeWorks employees: Danny Yoder, Linda Hart, Sean Alberson, Mary Jonasen and Ed Petersen (top)
GroundWorks Landscaping Crew (middle)

The first dollar earned by HopeWorks in 2011

Reprise

All of these programs build on Housing Hope's quarter century of dedicated effort, and were born out of a deep discussion at the 2010 strategic planning retreat. The board also dealt with leadership continuity by addressing the important issue of succession. A deputy executive director position was created to enhance internal leadership opportunities and development. This new assignment was created in part to accommodate Ed's focus on HopeWorks and community development activities, and in part as a response to Kathleen Horner's urging of leadership development. Furthermore, a process for leadership succession on the board was instituted. A three-year leadership plan was created in which a board member was elected as vice president with the understanding that they would become the president the following year, and the outgoing president would remain on the executive committee another year as past president. In this way the executive committee had three leaders serving at all times, providing strong organizational continuity.

The veritable explosion of ideas and energy that came toward the end of the decade coincided with the renewal of the agency's building program under its subsequent board presidents. Paul Vexler, founder and CEO of Quantum Windows and Doors, served as president for a year after Kathleen Horner's departure in July of 2009. It was a difficult time, the absolute nadir of the housing and financial collapse, and it was accompanied by complaints from a neighbor about residents at one of Housing Hope's facilities. Though these complaints were likely fed by the anxiety of the times, some of them played out in the media. At one point Paul suffered stoically through a questioning session convened by Everett's Mayor and Police Chief at a meeting to discuss residents hanging out on the sidewalks in front of a business establishment in downtown Everett. Paul patiently worked through any issues that arose and focused on strategic priorities. One of these led Paul to help get Taproot consultation services in Seattle to provide five human resource experts to volunteer and assist Housing Hope in developing its first ever Human Resources strategic plan.

Group 25 of the sweat equity home ownership program included five members of the Tulalip Tribes who built their homes over two winters at a site named Mission Highlands on the Tulalip Reservation, the first USDA-funded Self Help project that Housing Hope had built on tribal lands. At one time the builders had to work through two feet of snow. When the houses were done, Tulalip Tribal Singers offered blessings of prayer and song at the key ceremony in support of the commitment and accomplishments of these tribal members.

'y at Mission Highlands

ı year of ser-
ɔny Hatch is
ntly elected
Board mem-
ressed pride
to be part of
ıoment.
an exciting
of families,"
t means that
hen you can
f yourself to
'hese people
to get their
ɔr what they
ıe work ethic
ng."
Iope Execu-
Ed Petersen
at his orga-
al is to help
houses and
, by giving
owner-build-
ɔ, not a hand-
ner-builders
work Oct.
ster a sense
ty between
re required
each other's
y have liter-
ls of hours of
ıead of them
ill be allowed
til everyone's
completed.

ING page A2

KIRK BOXLEITNER The Marysville Globe

Shelley and James "Snooks" Yant have already been working since Oct. 4, and look forward to the freedom that will come from finally having their own home.

Five Native American families built their homes on the Tulalip Reservation through Self Help Housing

The passage of the Housing and Economic Recovery Act by Congress in 2008 simplified funding for low-income housing, and the American Recovery and Reinvestment Act by Congress in 2010 helped low-income housing tax credit properties get additional financing. This finally loosened up the housing market that had been frozen for several years. By August of 2008 Group 26 had begun constructing the first homes at Copper Station, followed a year later by Groups 27, 28, by Group 29 in 2010 and 30 in 2011. Also in that year, the five families of Group 31 began constructing their houses at Marvin Gardens in Monroe.

Housing Hope theme: constructing housing solutions

Norming Housing Hope

Storming, Forming, Norming is nomenclature from organizational development literature. Organizations go through phases of development. The initial storming phase is the startup period and is filled with urgency to do something about an agreed upon problem. It involves brainstorming, idealistic hopes and creative ideas. This is followed by the forming phase during which operating structure is defined. By-laws, incorporation, election of officers, establishment of goals and selection of projects and development of business plans occur.

Norming is the process by which the rules and protocols of an organization are integrated into the corporate culture. Systems for staff and board communication are established and the role of each in pursuing corporate goals is solidified. Systems are set up; goals and objectives are established and reporting systems put in place to measure progress. Routines emerge and things happen in predictable ways. At Housing Hope this storming, forming, norming progression is seen in the development of Action Committees, the creation of separate agencies, the movement of property management to Coast Real Estate, the development of branch boards and the creation of board leadership succession.

An interesting recent exploration about a key norm was the issue of merit pay. The organization had developed a family-like culture that fostered a high level of staff commitment to excellence. This culture tapped the intrinsic motivation of staff to contribute to the mission of the organization because, being values-driven, they believed their work addressed a significant community problem and their effort made a difference. When merit pay was introduced as a best practice in the corporate business sector, a debate ensued. Shouldn't the highest achieving employees be rewarded monetarily for their contributions to organizational success? On the other hand, was organizational success a by-product of collective wisdom and energy which could be undermined by rewarding some individuals and not others? There were those that argued that almost all of the employees are high achievers, a result of effective recruitment together with an empowering work environment. The risk that the "norming" achieved by the organization might be unraveled by merit pay, and that teamwork and collective wisdom could be threatened by introducing a new compensation system, was carefully considered by staff leaders and board members. Ultimately the board determined that Housing Hope was not ready for a merit pay system

Housing Hope also refined the ways it screened and selected employees. Bruce Eklund tells the insightful story about using the technique of behavioral interviewing. In this process applicants are given a list of questions to study, about how they have dealt with issues and events in their past. In one case, the written responses of applicants applying for the position of asset analyst, in which all candidates save one had experience, led the agency to select the one with no experience, Bobby Thompson. His responses indicated that he would better fit the Housing Hope culture. His non-technical skills, enthusiasm to learn and excellent communication skills made him the stronger choice despite his lack of technical experience. His excellent work with Housing Hope since joining the staff in 2009 has proved the technique's worth.

Housing Hope grew up with the dotcom revolution and has kept pace with rapid technological change. In its earlier and poorer years, the agency's technology platform evolved slowly and items were added only if needed or as they were donated. John Sevy was instrumental in getting the agency to think about increasing its technological capacity with the result that every employee in the main office got a computer plus training in Word and Excel. In 1997 Mel Southwick installed a state-of-the-art phone system and wired HHV for the future. When Bruce Eklund became Housing Hope's Chief Operating Officer in 2006, he and continued to build its capacity.

Housing Hope's experiences during the dark days of the Great Recession reaffirmed many of its financial strategies. The collapse of the housing bubble had positive as well as negative effects. On the positive side, properties the agency desired to acquire became cheaper. The negative effect was that properties the agency owned fell in value, particularly a problem for properties in the process of development, where appraised values were critical. Also, properties the agency owned fell in value. The failure of the Federal Home Loan Mortgage Corporation (Freddie Mac) and the Federal National Mortgage Association (Fannie Mae) together with the broader banking crisis caused the market for low-income housing tax credits to collapse. Bankers were unable to or refused to make loans and housing construction came to a halt. The Federal Stimulus Package provided special funding to make up for the lost tax credits, but in the case of Lincoln Hill Village, this did not help.

The Lincoln Hill Village (LHV) became the poster child of just how wrong things could go. The property Housing Hope sought to purchase went on the market near the height of the housing boom. The sales process became an auction as bidders upped their offers. Housing Hope had been pursuing a property purchase in Stanwood for four years and was thrilled to finally succeed in acquiring a suitable site for a multifamily development. The agency proposed to finance the project through its now typical use of 9% low-income housing tax credits. In fierce competition for the credits, their proposal was not successful. Enter Plan B. The project was restructured using "non-competitive" 4% tax credit/tax exempt bonds. The 9% tax credit application required that 75% of the village's units be occupied by homeless families, but the 4% tax credit/tax exempt bonds did not. However, the project was delayed for a year while waiting for a tax-exempt bond allocation from the State. During this delay, the economy collapsed and the sale of tax credits was no longer viable. Enter Plan C. In the American Recovery and Reinvestment Act of 2010, Congress provided alternatives to tax credit financing. Unfortunately, these funds were devoted to resurrecting 9% tax credit projects, and Lincoln Hill Village had already been converted to 4% tax credits. And finally, Plan D. In addition to Lincoln Hill Village, Housing Hope had another partially funded multi-family project on its hands: Woods Creek Village in Monroe. Both projects had been awarded grants by state and county agencies. Rather than have both projects languish, the agency succeeded in getting the state and county to aggregate their grants and apply them solely to Lincoln Hill Village. A capital campaign raised $876,600 from a host of donors including the Peter Henning Junior family of Stanwood. For their generosity, the village's community building was named The Henning Family Learning Center. And when Peter introduced Floyd Jones to this Stanwood project, which was being built

Henning Family Learning Center at Lincoln Hill Village (above)
Delores & Floyd Jones courtyard at Lincoln Hill Village (left)

Photos courtesy of Designs Northwest

blocks from where his deceased wife Delores grew up and went to school, Floyd also made a generous donation, and the space at the center of the project was named the Delores and Floyd Jones Courtyard.

For the first time in Housing Hope's history, a housing development of the organization was bestowed with artwork. Architect Dan Nelson approached Camano Island artist Jack Archibald, who donated a stained glass work titled "Rise up Singing" with glass pieces for each of the four sides of the Henning building. Jack described the title as, "well..... it's that line in summertime, 'one of these mornings you're going to rise up singing, then you'll spread your wings and you'll take to the sky.' Just sort of an optimism that seemed contagious and maybe appropriate for your project, where hopefully folks will get the opportunity for a fresh start. I wanted the design to be uplifting, literally and metaphorically." Wood sculptor Paul Vexler donated a helix creation, which was hung prominently facing the street in the Learning Center. Architect Dan Nelson and artist Jack Gunter teamed up to produce a storyboard to mount in the Learning Center, documenting the Peter Henning Senior migration in 1883 from famine in Sweden to prosperity in Stanwood. Housing Hope learned again what it always knew, that the corporate norms were strong because they included doggedness around setting clear goals, being flexible in attaining them, but most importantly remembering that first efforts don't always succeed and one must not be easily discouraged by obstacles along the way. And also importantly, following the money trail didn't necessarily lead to long term success. More important still were the relationships nurtured with the communities Housing Hope served. If these were healthy and strong, the vagaries of finance were of secondary concern. The adage "where there's a will, there's a way" is apt. And in the end Lincoln Hill Village turned out to be a beautiful home for 24 low-income and homeless families.

And Still More Presidents

Sarah Duncan followed Paul Vexler as board president, serving from July of 2010 to June of 2011. A star basketball player in high school, she attended and played at the University of Washington and earned a law degree, later partnering in the law firm of Tom Adams, a longtime friend of Housing Hope. She was brought onto the board because she was bright and young, younger even than Todd Morrow when Housing Hope was founded. Integrating the next generation in the work of Housing Hope was important. Another addition of youth was added when 28-year-old Julie Kestle, formerly a homeless teen mom, was recruited to serve on the board. Sarah oversaw the opening of Mt. Baker View including its Ten Degrees college-going environment and Lincoln Hill Village, as well as the acquisition of Park Place Townhomes, a 14 unit development in Marysville and the startup of the HopeWorks nonprofit agency.

In July of 2011, Jimmy Yamauchi became president of the board. A native of Hawaii, he was working for GTE, the telephone company, when Hurricane Iniki devastated service on his island of Kauai in 1992. Confronting immediate needs with no resources, he sat down with his area managers and brainstormed a process that restored 95% of service within ten weeks. The experience served him well. During an earlier stint on the Housing Hope board, he had led the creative effort to convert Stone Soup into a signature fundraising event. In July 2012 Robert Walker becomes Board President to end the first 25 years and begin the second 25 years.

Once again Housing Hope had picked up speed, planning significant new 'villages' in Monroe and Smokey Point, and expanding Tomorrow's Hope into a full-fledged child development center. A strong board was complemented by a dedicated and highly effective staff leadership team. Amongst these were Diane Smith who began as receptionist and 16 years later ran

Julie's Story

How do you give voice to those who seek and utilize Housing Hope programs? One way was to maintain a spot on the board of directors for someone who had been served by the agency.

Julie Kestle

In November 2000 Julie was a scared, destitute and desperate 18-year-old homeless mom with a five-month-old baby. She had learned what it was like caring for an infant in a car and was tired of it. Somehow, she landed at Housing Hope, moved into a small one-bedroom apartment and began building a life for her child. As Julie's life stabilized, she volunteered as a receptionist for Housing Hope, was selected as a live-in resident manager at Avanti House for teen moms and eventually was hired by the Housing Hope property management program.

Julie parlayed her training and work experience at Housing Hope into property management jobs at various agencies, and in 2012 manages a 150-unit apartment complex with 30 homeless family units. She knows and understands these families, which makes her the perfect property manager for them.

In November 2010, on the 10th anniversary of her entry as a resident into the Housing Hope program, Julie Kestle was elected to the Housing Hope board of directors.

the internal office and daily administrative operations and Bruce Eklund who brought new internet and technology capabilities to Housing Hope. When they retired in 2011 good succession plans allowed the organization to not miss a beat. Good leadership would be key to the future because, although, in 2012, the combined efforts of Housing Hope and other nonprofits have created a strong housing program for the homeless population in the County, every year at least 2000 homeless families come forward asking for help.

...And Finally

In 25 years Housing Hope has accomplished a great deal. It has helped thousands of homeless families put their lives back together and prepare for productive futures, and it has helped their children learn and grow. All in all, in 25 years that is no small potatoes.

Peter Henning

It is through Peter Henning that this writer comes into the story. I met Peter in 2001 when I agreed to write a biography of his father, Peter Henning senior, a Swedish immigrant to Washington, who helped build the Great Northern's tracks through Stevens Pass, made a small fortune in Alaska during the gold rush then came back to invest it in Everett real estate. He founded the community of East Stanwood, raised his family there and helped grow Snohomish County. Having finished that book I convinced Peter Henning Jr. that he was at least as interesting as his father and deserved a biography of his own. He grew up in Stanwood, raised an award-winning herd of Jersey cattle and became an influential dairy farmer. When he tired of dairy politics he decided to go back to college and become a nuclear physicist. He explored the interior structure of the element tantalum and was instrumental in convincing oncologists to make use of linear accelerators in the treatment of cancer. It was when I was researching his later role as a property developer, his explorations of the Silk Road, and his philanthropies that he mentioned his recent experience of, in his words, being blown away by Ed Petersen's descriptions of Housing Hope's mission and work.

When Ed told him he wanted to find someone to write Housing Hope's history for its 25th anniversary, Peter mentioned me. In 2011, during our exploratory conversations I told Ed a good institutional history would require a year of research and a year to write. Ed thought six months should be sufficient, and I learned first-hand what people mean when they say how difficult it is to say no to Ed. As to the quality of this history I leave that to the reader. Even as I write these words in the Housing Hope offices I can hear Ed's swift, long-legged stride clomp, clomp, clomping down the hall and see him burst into the room, tall and still slim in jeans, an open throat shirt and sport jacket, a wispy beard grayer for his 25 years at the helm, but still a person who exudes the enthusiasm and drive that helped to make Housing Hope what it is.

Photographs of the buildings Housing Hope has erected and of the people they serve are on view in its main office beside Pigeon Creek, if anyone needs convincing. One image I have always found riveting: a mother with her arms around her three adolescent children looks resolutely into the eye of the camera; her children look just as resolutely away. The present may be much better, but the memories of their past are still painful.

A new generation of givers must be cultivated. And beyond those who are likely to give, there are those who ask why they should support programs that serve the needs of those who either didn't do what was needed or made bad choices. Bad luck is one thing, but those who are asked to give a hand up...., well, who gave them one when they struggled through school, worked hard to get good grades, worked hard in crappy jobs to get better ones, bought a fixer-upper and are still trying to fix it up? Who helped them when they lived poor and took on debt to raise their children to be well educated and self-sufficient? They didn't make the wrong decisions; they didn't break the law, they didn't become alcoholics or drug addicts. Why should they give?

"They are not always easy to serve," Ed admits, describing the homeless, but adds, "there is great satisfaction in reaching out to those who've hit rock bottom and desperately want a better future." "We may not like the filth they are forced to live in," cautions Todd Morrow, "but they are still people." Connie Wittren, the director of resource development at Housing Hope in the '90s, offered her practical insight: "[Surviving] Homelessness requires tenacity, creativity, and incredible resourcefulness, all of which are transferrable skills. Human potential is a renewable resource which can compete with any tangible element, yet so much has been left to rot on humanity's dust heap."

The argument for giving is not always an easy one to make. And as we do so, we should remember there are other, older reasons given for extending the hand of compassion, reasons that resonate within ancient and treasured messages passed down to us that bid us to reflect on what it means to be fully human. These urge us to be generous for our own sake, and point to the depth of pain inflicted when we are not.

For I was hungry and you gave me food, I was thirsty and you gave me drink, a stranger and you welcomed me, naked and you clothed me, ill and you cared for me, in prison and you visited me. Then the righteous will answer him and say, 'Lord, when did we see you hungry and feed you, or thirsty and give you drink? When did we see you a stranger and welcome you, or naked and clothe you? When did we see you ill or in prison and visit you? And the King will say to them in reply, 'Amen I say to you, whatever you did for one of the least of these brothers and sisters of mine, you did for me'.

The girl sleepily carried the stuffed animals from the motel to the waiting car. Her older brother was already asleep in the back seat and her mother helped her in and buckled her seat belt. The motel room smelled of stale cigarettes and unwashed clothes; the

Housing Hope Services Provided in 2010

Figures taken from 2010 Annual Report

Emergency Shelters

103
Individuals served

6,078
Bed nights provided

Transitional Housing

526
Individuals served

126,368
Bed nights provided

Permanent Housing

162
Apartments operated

196
Families served

Rebranded Team Homebuilding in 2011

Self Help Housing

14
Houses started

21
Houses completed

110
Individuals served

cold car smelled of mildew, but the heater warmed the air and the girl fell asleep. When she awoke, she looked at her animals and noticed the bunny was missing. "Mom!" she cried out; "Bunny's missing! He's back at the apartment!" Over the rush of the car her mother answered, "I'm sorry honey, we can't go back. Mama will get you a new one." The little girl cried herself back to sleep. She would never forget the bunny. All her life she would remember the soft, tender thing that became the symbol for everything she would lose.

As Housing Hope enters its next twenty-five years, much work remains. Whatever the causes of homelessness, its impact on adults is humiliating and debilitating. But its impact on children, who are blameless and who require love, care and stability, is crushing. Their suffering opens a great wound in the body politic. Compassion and common sense inform us that the effort to end homelessness is a far better use of our resources than trying to heal its awful consequences. To this end the heart and soul of those who carry out Housing Hope's mission must continually be reinvigorated with ingenuity, strategic initiative and determination. As the need persists, its work will continue in Snohomish County, and we call on those who read about Housing Hope in these pages to reflect on its success and the need. We offer our history as a template to those who would work to end homelessness in their areas, to shelter families, to offer a hand up to those who need it and to ensure that children no longer have to suffer unnecessary loss.

David M. Buerge
August 15, 2012

Children's Programs

200
Individuals served

20,566
Days of childcare provided

In Education & Life Skills

484
Individuals served

4,117
Classroom instructional hours provided.

Additionally, Housing Hope provided basic health insurance to 275 individuals. In 25 years Housing Hope has built six shelter units, nearly 125 units of homeless family transitional housing and over 200 units of low-income permanent housing. It has taught 238 families to build their own homes, helping them to become homeowners.

Epilogue *by William H. Gates, Sr.*

Beginning with the early days of the Pacific Northwest, Building Hope tells the story of how a community was formed and shaped by hard work, determination and faith. It is a remarkable story. It is made all the more remarkable by the struggles faced by several generations of residents who had to ride out the ups and downs that buffeted a new community and economy.

The story of the cycles of housing instability and homelessness is an essential part of any honest account of who we are, where we have come from, and the issues that we must continue to address. Building Hope, and the history of Housing Hope, details the essential role played by concerned citizens in Snohomish County as they tackled this issue. Initially driven by the strong faith with deep roots in the Northwest's Scandinavian tradition, Housing Hope has become a symbol of the best our communities can be as they mobilize effective responses to the needs of individuals and families who are struggling with circumstances substantially beyond their control.

Although family homelessness is nothing new, the recession of the 1980's created a unique problem in this country. For the first time, as the economy recovered, wages did not keep pace with the cost of housing, and families that had been hit hardest were unable to keep their housing. The significant increase in family homelessness led to the rise of a crisis response from government and non-profit partners. This response resulted in a growing network of family shelters.

Early on, Housing Hope recognized that shelters alone were insufficient and temporary in addressing the problem. If we were to end family homelessness, more enduring solutions that supported families as they returned to stability were required. Moving beyond shelter, Housing Hope embraced a model that included both transitional and permanent housing.

But their efforts did not stop there. Housing Hope also recognized that affordable, safe and decent housing needed to be accompanied by economic stability for families. This required skills to ready parents for employment, as well as access to child care for the children of hard working parents. The College of Hope, Hope Works, and the licensed child care services Housing Hope developed and continues to provide are models for how an organization with a vision can make changes happen for families.

At the Bill & Melinda Gates Foundation, we are driven by two basic principles: That every life has equal value, and that every person should have the opportunity to live a healthy and productive life. Whether we are working to eradicate polio in the developing world, or tackling extreme poverty in our own local communities, we are committed to tackling what others have too often labeled "intractable" social problems.

After a careful analysis of the greatest inequities facing families in our region, the foundation joined the work of ending family homelessness through the Sound Families Initiative in 2000. Working in Snohomish, King and Pierce counties, the foundation invested $42M to develop transitional and permanent housing linked with supportive services for families recovering from homelessness. In Snohomish County, Housing Hope was a lead partner, developing new units of transitional housing that allowed them to build on the hard work of their already well-established organization. Through effective leadership and strong management, Housing Hope became an effective embodiment of the foundation's efforts to promote solutions to homelessness for families. We are proud to consider Housing Hope our partner and our friend.

In 2007, we paused in our Sound Families work to assess our progress. Although we had helped to successfully house more than 1500 families and provide increased stability for more than 2800 children, we were troubled by the fact that we had not made any measurable progress in reducing the overall rates of family homelessness in our communities. In fact, between 2000 and 2007, the problem had gotten worse, rather than better. Although three-quarters of the families exiting from Sound Families made successful transitions to permanent housing, more and more families were waiting in line for what was continuing to be an insufficient supply of affordable housing resources.

In 2009, working together with the Washington Families Fund under the leadership of Building Changes, a strong local non-profit intermediary, we began focusing on the systems dysfunction that seem to lie at the core of this issue.

We now believe that permanently re-housing families that are in crisis and linking them to the services and supports they need to stabilize offers the best pathway to ending homelessness. Each of the public sector systems and non-profit providers that touch these families must develop the capacities to work together to address each family's strengths and needs. Whether families are involved with the child welfare or domestic violence systems; whether they have educational needs or severe mental illnesses; whether they require a short-term, shallow subsidy or intensive services paired with permanent housing – every partner working to address the needs of homeless families must align their work, their resources and their energies in ways that support and move families towards the goals and outcomes each family prioritizes.

Housing Hope was early to the table in recognizing the need for an individually tailored response to each family's situation. They have led Snohomish County and many other communities to the current stage of our journey.

We look forward to our continued partnership with Housing Hope as we work together to direct our skills and our energies towards the systems level changes that have the potential to transform each family's journey out of homelessness and towards the stability and self-sufficiency that should be within the reach of every American.

As we think back to the pioneering spirit that created Washington State, Snohomish County, and ultimately Housing Hope, we must also continue to look to the work that lies ahead. The history of Housing Hope provides an inspiration to us all in how to make change happen.

William H. Gates, Sr.
Founding Executive Director, Bill and Melinda Gates Foundation

William H. Gates, Sr. is a retired attorney and philanthropist. He guides the vision, strategic direction and serves as an advocate for the Foundation's key issues.

Chapter 3169 of the Great Northwest Harley Owners Group (H.O.G.) celebrate their 19th annual Bunny Run, bringing gifts, funds and compassion for homeless children on Easter Weekend 2012

Integrating Harley riders with the Easter Bunny and homeless children is "out of the box thinking". The above picture is a metaphor for bringing a community together to create housing solutions and provide vital services for homeless and low-income families with children.

Both require vision and management in tandem with resources sufficient to the task.

Appendix *The Housing Hope Model*

Questions with Answers by Ed Petersen

Vision:

Housing Hope's Vision Statement is, "All individuals aspiring to self-sufficiency should have access to an affordable home."

Q. Is vision really important?

A. Defining the problem is the first step toward action to solve the problem. The second step is to visualize the solution. Organizations develop vision statements as a way of concretely framing their solution. By doing this a north star for navigating the work of an organization is defined. The vision should serve as the inspiration for action. Ideally it galvanizes participants for the hard work, sacrifice and challenges which are essential to achieving lofty aspirations.

When an organization assembles many people and has many activities underway, it is easy to lose focus on the mission. Gaining consensus on priorities and directions becomes more difficult as complexity of operations and demands grow. A vision statement brings the organization together for coordinated collective action toward achieving outcomes that are significant.

Q. How has Housing Hope's vision statement affected its model?

A. Housing Hope was founded because of a problem in the marketplace. Housing was not affordable. The vision statement adopted by the agency combines two elements, one micro and the other macro.

The individual is at the center of the micro perspective. It was the pathos from story after story of individuals striving for a better future that touched the founders and leaders of Housing Hope. Individuals were trying hard and families wanted to provide better for their children. Time after time we heard aspirations to be self-sufficient. But they were constantly being stymied.

The macro element is housing economics. The affordability of housing is determined by decisions in our society. Every country handles this basic need for shelter differently. In our country the cost of housing floats with supply and demand and is affected by public policy and capital incentives. A safe, secure, affordable home for all is not elevated to a pre-ordinate value in the United States. The US economic system promotes and subsidizes homeownership through the tax code. However, support is absent for market rate rental housing and weak for the housing needs of low-income and homeless households. Housing Hope's vision statement sets the agency at odds with these societal priorities, and advocates for a home for all who seek to be self-sufficient.

Together these two views set the framework for Housing Hope's model. The resulting mission statement was created to address both the micro and macro elements of this vision statement.

Mission:

"Housing Hope shall promote and provide a continuum of safe, decent, affordable housing and necessary related services for very low and low-income residents of Snohomish County and Camano Island."

Q. How was this mission statement created and how does it relate to outcomes achieved?

A. The Board of Directors spent considerable time discussing the mission statement. Since the agency had been created as a Housing Development Corporation the intent was to assemble special expertise for the development of affordable housing. Early in this discussion, however, a series of game-changing questions were framed:

- Is quantity of housing produced more important than quality? In other words, should the Housing Hope create as many sleeping accommodations (emergency shelter with lots of beds) as quickly as possible in response to the large homeless population?
- What income segment of the population in need should be targeted?
- What geography should be targeted?
- Should the focus be on production of housing or advocacy for housing?
- Should Housing Hope limit itself to one type of housing or one population?
- Should Housing Hope limit itself to housing or include service delivery as well?

The resulting mission statement, developed carefully with active participation of all Board Members and staff leaders, answered these six questions.

The decision that each housing unit would be part of a comprehensive approach to help recipients toward self-sufficiency shaped the nature of the Housing Hope model for the next 25 years. The phrase "continuum of safe, decent, affordable housing" resulted from this debate. The idea was to create a real solution one household at a time with the belief that over time the quantity of housing would grow into a significant countywide, sustainable program of housing and connected services. The 25-year history of Housing Hope has demonstrated the viability of this belief.

Q. Why are the words in this statement important?

A. Housing Hope chose to consciously elevate "promote solutions" to a high level in its mission, because alone the agency will never produce enough units to eliminate the need. The knowledge gained in the practice of developing and operating affordable housing should be seen as a community asset (not as a competitive advantage) available to the broader community, with the goal of creating community conditions which will help solve the affordable housing crisis.

Temporary housing is a band-aid approach to addressing homelessness. In response to this understanding Housing Hope settled on the idea of a "housing continuum". The idea was to start with each household, destitute or just distressed, wherever they are when they enter the agency's program, and help them move to their optimum level of independent and sustainable housing. This continuum has been a work in progress for 25 years.

"Affordable" housing means that the household has money left after paying rent and utilities sufficient to buy food, clothes, medicine, provide transportation and meet the other essential needs of the members of the household.

The word "necessary" is interesting. If the agency wanted to strictly be a housing agency this word wouldn't be in the mission statement. But Housing Hope is really an anti-poverty agency. It utilizes housing as a means toward other ends. These ends are self-sufficiency and thriving families. Necessary related services are those that help end homelessness for families and residents. Judgment is needed to determine which services are really necessary to achieve this end. Metrics and program evaluation are utilized to determine what is really essential.

Housing Hope has not shied away from the daunting challenge of being both service experts and housing experts. This is noteworthy. Most agencies do one or the other. And most housing agencies focus on one type of housing in order to become known as experts in this product. Housing Hope chose a different path.

The "lowest income segment" of the community was identified as the target population in the Housing Hope founding documents. At the same time, it was understood that choosing to serve a higher income population could, at times, be a means to serve extremely low income individuals. From the beginning a careful distinction between ends and means has been maintained. To date 99% of the almost 600 units produced by Housing Hope serve low- and very low-income households.

Organizational Development:
The right people on the bus.

Q. What organizing principles were utilized in the startup of Housing Hope?

A. None Of Us Has All The Answers. "Learn from experience" was the first principle. There was no grand theoretical framework that guided our organizational development. We began with the knowledge that other communities had created successful housing development corporations. There were good models to learn from and the successes of others were taken as an inspiration. Our task was to figure out how the same kind of results could be achieved in the unique Snohomish County environment.

This first principle also led to our belief in collective wisdom. None of us is as smart as all of us together. A healthy process involving many produces unique perspectives, new ideas, creative solutions and most importantly engages the broader team in a sense of ownership for the direction or decision taken.

Right Is Might. The old adage that "might is right" is turned on its head, as it was in Camelot, and became our second principal. We organized around the conviction that what we were doing was right. It was how to do it well, that needed to be learned. To believe intensely that provision of safe, secure affordable housing was the "right thing to do" brought individual and group energy. Providing affordable housing for the poor was consistent with the biblical mandate to have compassion for the poor and consistent with the New Testament message to put faith into action. There were also strong social and economic arguments in support of fulfilling this need. Government wanted to provide funds that would produce real solutions. Faith communities wanted to support our goals. The belief that something is right is a powerful and contagious ingredient. Holding tightly to the principle that we were doing the right thing as a group, our commitment to drawing new people into this conviction became a driving force for Housing Hope's development.

Accountability Earns Support. Our third principle was accountability. Housing Hope wanted to be good stewards of every gift received. Establishing a track record of accountability was at the heart of the long-term strategy for sustainability and growing success. The accountability principle applied to residents to be served as well. The agency mantra was a "hand up, not a hand out". Resident growth was conceptualized as a partnership in which progress achieved through individual effort was supported and applauded without producing dependency.

The Community Wants Vision and Good Management. The huge cost involved in the issue of affordable housing was daunting and caused many to step up to the issue and then walk away. The issue of homeless families with children was hugely complex. The costly and complex nature of these issues existed in the context of a community that wanted solutions. People and institutions were poised to lend support if a good, compelling and viable model could be created. Housing Hope stepped up with its vision of a Service Enriched Housing Continuum and its ability to manage resources. With opportunities to contribute in the form of time, talent or treasure, those who wanted to be part of the solution now had a viable avenue to channel their support.

Q. What organizational development stages has Housing Hope experienced?

A. Storming was the first. At the beginning with no track record, no financing and no mentors, the task was to be creative. Board members were very active during this stage in discussing plans in detail and helping with program implementation. Board members went door-to-door to inform neighbors about our first facility, recruited groups to adopt apartments, provided needed items for residents and acted as a speaker's bureau for presentations to community groups. The Board organized work parties, arranged for Housing Hope logo design, assisted with grant applications, spoke to funders and arranged annual dinners in church basements to celebrate accomplishments. All hands were on board and they were busy wherever opportunity might arise.

Forming follows storming. As time passed and progress toward goals was realized, the complexity of the organization made it more difficult to be quite so spontaneous. Systems for decision making, documentation and messaging emerged. The staff was responsible for maintaining these systems. Priorities for projects and for staff time began to emerge. A structure for Board involvement evolved around committees of the Board. The first standing committees were organized around housing, finance and strategic planning. Other committees followed for social services, resource development and human resources. These committees were designed to prepare policy recommendations for Board action and to provide technical assistance to staff. In this way the technical know-how of board members and their community connections could still benefit the agency, and board member involvement could be strategically tailored.

Norming follows forming. Staff members triggered further development of structure with the request to add predictability to the work environment. There was a need to know the rules and understand the parameters of each position, program and initiative. Eventually, personnel policies and finance procedures and fiscal policies were put in writing with greater detail. Leadership team meetings, called the Directors Council, were scheduled on a regular biweekly basis and all-staff meetings were held monthly as a vehicle to keep everyone informed and to foster a team spirit in the midst of continuing rapid growth and constant change. Organizational values became better articulated. Boundaries between departments of the agency became clearer and a culture of teamwork was developed.

Over time, the dependence on the founding Executive Director was reduced as norms became embedded in the fabric of the organization. The need to be creative at every turn had evolved into an institution that possessed solid problem-solving skills and program delivery at every level, guided by strong leaders and well-established norms. By the 25th year, Housing Hope had earned the respect of the community for producing solid results year in and year out.

Q. How does Housing Hope think about staff development?

A. Staff development must be understood in the context of the organizational environment. Housing Hope's model is that work should be uplifting and meaningful. Collective talent and commitment is assembled by the agency to address one of the significant social ills of our day: children and their families and individuals who have no home or may lose their home. Staff members are seen as integral to the agency's success in solving family homelessness and the crisis of affordable housing.

Technical knowledge and skill is essential to the success of the agency. It's the program director level that is at the heart of creating and energizing an effective work environment. From inception there were four key competency areas at Housing Hope: housing, services, fundraising and finance. Today the strategic plan describes these as affordable housing, supportive services, resource development, social enterprise and administration. Each of these fields is vital to mission success for the organization. The leaders of these departments need to be technically competent and skilled at collaboration. These individuals are the key to creation and maintenance of the kind of work environment conducive to organizational success.

Using Jim Collins concept of "members on the bus" as articulated in his book Good to Great, Housing Hope seeks to recruit, retain and develop a team of individuals who share common values and commitments. Members refer to staff and board. Bus refers to the Housing Hope organization. The most important staff quality sought in recruitment is passion for the mission. Beyond that, personal attitudes and skills that energize the work environment are sought. These include good communication skills, hunger to learn, belief in the importance of collaboration, compassion and a healthy balance of listening and teaching skills. Once we have the right members, our team leaders can teach the technical knowledge and skills. The cases where there has been poor employee performance are typically due to a poor match, where employee personal qualities don't resonate with the work environment to produce positive energy.

Promotion from within into leadership positions has increasingly become a key to program success. Staff members within the organization who have demonstrated the personal qualities conducive to effectiveness have the opportunity to grow into leaders. Housing Hope has been regularly successful in teaching leadership where the ground is fertile.

Staff development funding is budgeted annually for staff members to attend workshops and training. This provides a complement to internal training provided on the job through organizational leaders.

Q. Is Board development important to Housing Hope's success?

A. First and foremost, Board Members are the "stakeholders" who represent the community in governing the corporation. The charitable purpose of the agency is commemorated in writing through the Articles of Incorporation and Bylaws. The Internal Revenue Service has reviewed these documents and bestowed upon Housing Hope a charitable purpose and a right to receive philanthropic support which entitles donors to receive a tax benefit. The Board of Directors serves as guardians of this charitable purpose and is accountable to the IRS for compliance. Training to perform this function well has been an important Board development agenda since the first United Way-sponsored Board training event in 1989.

Members are also recruited and elected to the Board for two other purposes: technical expertise and community connections. Real Estate development is complex. The first members the founders added to the Board had backgrounds in fields such as asset management, real estate, private lending, property development and law. Consumers and social service professionals were brought onto the Board for the unique experiential perspective they possessed; later, marketing experts were added to assist the organization in better telling its story. These experts brought richness to the Board discussions and helped educate their colleagues as the Board carried out its policy making tasks. In addition, technical assistance to the staff benefitted the growth of programs, systems and outcomes for the agency.

The founders of Housing Hope had strong connections to faith communities which were leveraged to engage many new congregations. They also brought connections to the criminal justice system, health care system and mental health system. From its inception the Board was clear about key connections needed in the community for success. Recruitment of new members was carefully managed to attract and retain individuals who would resonate with the mission of Housing Hope, especially with the commitment to the lowest income segment of the community and who would broaden the community connections in support of agency goals.

Training on effective boardsmanship has also been a focus from time to time. Occasional workshops have been held for the Board on risk management, legal responsibilities of Board Members, the advocacy role of Board Members and strategic planning. Because the Board functions so effectively, there has been only periodic priority put on these trainings.

Q. When and how did strategic planning enter the Housing Hope development?

A. Strategic plans were adopted by the Board from the very beginning. The original plans were very basic, consisting of a prioritized list of goals for the following year. It wasn't long before they became 3- and then 5-year goals. However, these were not well developed plans, and were lacking internal and external environment analysis. Nor were focused strategic questions identified or answered.

In 1995, Impact Capital determined that a capacity building effort around housing development would benefit the agency; Housing Hope's strategic planning became significantly more comprehensive and sophisticated. A grant was provided to fund an experienced planner who helped write a full strategic plan. Impact Capital knew that this would be a valuable tool toward presenting Housing Hope's case and convincing investors that Housing Hope plans had merit. The strategic plan called for the creation of a Housing Director position, with the intent that this would provide the essential technical know-how and housing development leadership for implementation of the plan.

In 2008, strategic planning evolved to a new level. Instead of adopting a new strategic plan every three or five years, it was decided to utilize a rolling strategic plan approach. Each year since then the Board of Directors convenes in March for its annual strategic planning retreat. The current year is removed and a new third year is added at the end of the two remaining years in the plan. Detailed plans for the first year of this new three year period are adopted, so that staff can put together an annual budget addressing these priorities.

Community Values:
A hand up, not a hand out.

Q. Why is "a hand up" such a driving force?

A. "A hand up" is a metaphor for one person helping another. It represents the idea that people care and that a community cares. A hand up connotes a meeting halfway between a person in need of and willing to receive help, and one who is willing and able to provide effective help. This is in contrast to a "hand out" which does not imply the same sense of community or relationship and does not stimulate personal initiative.

It's also a conceptual message to our residents, who have lost their way in the community. They are too often on the receiving end of relationships. Their extent of poverty is deep and they may have worn out their welcome with those they otherwise would turn to for help. As a result, they have little if any remaining natural support network, a critical resource for anyone in crisis. Rebuilding natural support networks where a genuine give-and-take relationship is present is an important focus for our residents. The concept of "a hand up" is embedded in the housing facilities created by Housing Hope. These are resident communities that build mutual support environments where each resident has opportunities to give others "a hand up".

Community buy-in of the Housing Hope mission is vital because the community provides the resources for the agency's success. Our community wants to help those who will help themselves. The use of the concept of "a hand up" resonates with our constituency. Using this terminology reinforces the view of Housing Hope supporters that the agency employs a model they can embrace. Community buy-in is a valuable intangible asset that is cultivated carefully by the Housing Hope messaging.

Q. How does Housing Hope address the issue of system abusers?

A. A system abuser is a person who has taken advantage of government subsidies, landlords, nonprofit agencies and others for personal gain. They have violated the terms and conditions of the help they've received or have manipulated the service system for benefits beyond the intended.

System abusers are a problem, because they undermine public trust in the honesty and integrity of individuals genuinely seeking help. Benefactors who have been taken advantage of by the abuser may become less charitable and compassionate as a result of this abuse. Other consumers - and our safety net system as a whole - suffer.

System abusers are usually victims. They have typically experienced terrible upbringings. Sometimes they've been victims of abuse, racism, prejudice or other discrimination. That said, when an individual approaches Housing Hope for help, our interest is in knowing if they are ready to change. We believe that the only avenue toward change is taking responsibility for one's behavior. Housing Hope seeks to help individuals who are willing to be held accountable. We seek to know and understand the person's past for two reasons. First, acknowledgement of one's past behavior is the essential first step toward change. Second, if the person is straightforward with us, we believe the motivation to work hard toward a different future is possible. Individual motivation to take necessary action is key to success.

One concrete strategy employed by Housing Hope is the use of a careful screening process at our Windermere Crossroads emergency shelter. During the first thirty-day stay, Housing Hope secures a landlord reference check, credit check, criminal history check and may send individuals for random urinalysis. We do this not to document and rule out those who have a checkered past. Rather, if what shows up on these background checks is the same as what the participant has told our staff it affirms our belief that there really is motivation to change. We see motivation to make changes as the key to our success in helping individuals overcome their past.

Organizational Philosophy:
We Keep Hope Alive

Q. Why does the agency use the word "hope" so often: Housing Hope, Tomorrow's Hope, College of Hope, Housing Hope Properties, HopeWorks Social Enterprises, HopeBuilders and Society of Hope?

A. Hope is the belief in things unseen. These hoped-for unseen things are dreams about the future. We dream about a future that will be successful and meaningful. Our dreams give us energy with which to do the hard work necessary to achieve fulfilling outcomes. That energy is hope. It is tragic when life circumstances deal a person such a blow that hope is crushed. When there is loss of hope, it's sad for the individual. But even more, it is sad for children whose future is profoundly impacted.

We put "hope" in our names for two reasons.

- It expresses our compassion. We care deeply

about each individual and each family that crosses our threshold. It expresses our willingness to walk with our residents and participants into a brighter future. And it expresses our belief that a brighter future is possible for those who work for it and utilize the support that is offered.

- It is about branding. We want it known all over the community that we are doing more than putting a roof over people's heads. We provide a comprehensive response to the assault on hope by infusing it in our buildings, our childcare program, our approach to life skills training and the way we address employment. Our innovative, multifaceted and targeted programs are well-known, both internally by our residents and externally in the community, because we are not shy about shouting our hope-oriented intentions to all corners of the county. We're about "hope".

Q. Who is the "we" in We Keep Hope Alive?

A. "We" is a lot of people, and this concept is absolutely fundamental to the Housing Hope model. It starts with the Board and its staff, and continues throughout the entire agency and its community.

These programs are only possible because of a community that cares. The time, talent and treasure provided by volunteers and donors are what make the service delivery feasible. Faith communities, who breathed life into the organization in 1987, and continue to do so, are part of the "we". Branch Boards, Supply Pantry volunteer groups and fundraising committees are also part of the "we", and so are corporate and student volunteer groups that provide work parties to support the Housing Hope sites and families. The "we" is a community of people who believe that every neighbor has value.

"It takes a village" has become a well known concept. Housing Hope purposely did not implement an expert paradigm at its inception, but rather sought to be a vehicle for community engagement in solving family homelessness.

Operational Model:

Housing Hope will be the best locally-based Service Enriched Housing Continuum for homeless families... in the world.

Q. Why has so much emphasis been placed on community involvement?

A. First, there are not enough resources to solve homelessness or affordable housing without community support. Second, collective wisdom is needed to find models that will succeed in the diverse areas of our county. In addition, sustainability of programs established by Housing Hope will be dependent on goodwill in the neighborhood and community. Third, the potential and likelihood of resistance to some Housing Hope program ideas is great, as stigma against some populations to be housed is strong.

Q. How has Housing Hope maintained such a high degree of collaboration with other agencies in an environment of competition for scarce resources?

A. Housing Hope put the word "promote" in its mission statement because it is committed to solving family homelessness and the affordable housing crisis. This will require the whole community working together. Housing Hope is a steward of insights and knowledge learned about these two issues. We have a responsibility to use this knowledge, working closely with others, to find broad community-wide strategies.

We know that safe, secure, affordable housing is the key to success for many social service agencies. When their clients are helped to find stable housing, these recipients are more likely to obtain the maximum benefits from the excellent counseling, education and other services programs that address their needs.

Housing Hope works hard to be a good partner with anyone who is concerned about family homelessness and affordable housing. This started in partnerships with faith communities. Government, corporate and philanthropic partnerships have been significant allies over the years.

More globally, Housing Hope has spent many years building up a very special environment of collaboration. This has been cultivated through affiliation agreements and memorandums of understanding with partner agencies for sharing service and housing resources. We are always willing to write support letters for other agencies when worthy projects are proposed. And Housing Hope and sister agencies jointly participate in committees, task forces and work groups to address housing and homelessness issues.

Q. Is community organizing skill essential to Housing Hope's success?

A. Community organizing is at the heart of our success. Understanding the community is the key to formulating strategies that will succeed. Community norms must be understood, power structures need to be identified, resources analyzed and tensions pinpointed. With a solid understanding of how the community system operates, an organizing effort can yield results. Being able to interpret the community system allows the community organizer to explain to participants what dynamics are at play in the project. This allows for the right kind of communication, education or advocacy to occur at the right time.

This rather theoretical statement about community organizing is a backdrop; relationships are the core of effective community organizing. Building a team of people who want to achieve results is the key. Whether it is advocacy for public policy changes or development of programs, effective community organizing fosters healthy relationships of people willing and able to collaborate.

Q. Why is there community involvement in each project development?

A. Each project needs goodwill and each project can benefit from maximizing supportive resources. Goodwill from a mayor, city council members, faith communities, neighbors and local funders is pivotal for each housing development.

Housing Hope has been more successful than most housing agencies in the state at raising philanthropic capital, startup financing and operating support for its developments and programs. This is due to its strong community connections. Philanthropic donors and foundations like being a part of an initiative that has broad community support.

Q. What components comprise Housing Hope's service-enriched housing continuum?

A. Shelter is linked to transitional housing which is linked to affordable rent housing and this is linked to home ownership. The housing continuum begins with 30- to 90-day emergency shelter. This is temporary housing for homeless families, and is designed to let families stabilize and begin planning for their future.

Shelter is connected to transitional housing, which is similar to affordable rental housing but includes additional service program assistance. Transitional housing may be used for stays of up to two years for families willing and desiring to be in a program to overcome current and potential future homelessness. Rent is set at 30% of income, and an array of services is wrapped around the housing. Each family develops an individualized family plan together with a case manager who meets with the head of household in their apartment weekly.

Transitional housing is linked to affordable rent housing. The agency considers this permanent housing in which the household can remain as long as they are in compliance with their lease. Some support services may be available, depending on the setting and needs of the family. Housing policies and housing program models have evolved and today the agency's portfolio of transitional housing is referred to as "rapid re-housing units".

For those families who are stable, have established a reliable income stream and maintain good credit, a sweat equity home ownership program is available through Housing Hope. This involves a group of families working together to build a group of houses with nobody getting the key to their home until all of the houses are complete. This program is designed for low income households who receive a subsidized loan through the US Department of Agriculture.

The "service enriched" part of the continuum includes a licensed childcare center dedicated to serving homeless families, a child development program for troubled or developmentally delayed children and their families, a life skills education program, employment services and case management support.

These housing types combined with wraparound services constitute Housing Hope's Service Enriched Housing Continuum.

Q. What are the ingredients for creating a collaborative community environment?

A. Willingness to listen is where it starts, and is the key to building relationships. Each person or institution comes forward out of their own needs or wants. Fundamentally, each wants to make a difference, but why and how they want to do this matters. Creating a collaborative environment involves taking what each party brings to the task and collectively finding a way to energize work together.

Community operates at many levels. It can be a congregation, a neighborhood or the entire county. The elements of collaborative environment will vary in each case. The skilled community worker learns how to operate on the boundaries where systems meet to find ways to foster increasingly overlapping purpose, communication and action. Social Workers are particularly suited to this work because they've been trained to understand systems and how they work. Moving from working with a family system to connecting that family to a public assistance system, for example, is an exercise in helping each of these systems understand the other and to adjust in order to achieve the ends of each. This is the skill a good practitioner uses to help healthy and successful collaborations succeed.

Housing Hope has mastered this art of bridging boundaries for successful collaborations.

Q. How did Housing Hope decide to commit to geographic distribution of its housing and service program?

A. We didn't want people in Everett, the county seat, to lose enthusiasm for supporting Housing Hope. Concerns were expressed that the agency programs might become a magnet that would bring large numbers of the homeless families to Everett. Such concerns were articulated in our early days. Assistance programs, by their very nature, attract service recipients to the locations where benefits are available. We did not want to pull homeless families from the entire county to congregate in Everett.

But more importantly, we understood that every household should have the option of staying in their home community, near family, schools, doctors and faith communities that serve as their social support systems. We also understood that the Washington Growth Management Act of 1990 required every jurisdiction to develop a Housing Element in their Comprehensive Plan that quantified the housing needs of all households in the jurisdiction and developed a strategy for how to address the needs of each income level.

We also understood that supporters and donors wanted to be involved in their home community. They wanted to see an impact on the needs of their neighbors who were destitute and reaching for a hand up. Housing Hope chose to be embedded in local communities where local citizens could help fashion and nurture solutions because we knew the impact, both real and perceived, would be greater.

Q. How has Housing Hope been able to succeed in serving the lowest income segment of the community?

A. Housing is expensive and those who build housing rely on sales or rental income to support the success of their development. Housing Hope has been tenacious in the face of challenges, and has utilized a multifaceted approach including:

- Grants from city, county, state and federal sources that reduce the amount of debt a housing development must carry.
- Housing Authority partnerships in which project-based subsidies enhance rental income.
- Grants from the Sound Families Initiative of the Bill and Melinda Gates Foundation which have provided capital and services funding for many projects.
- Philanthropic support from Windermere and Washington Mutual Bank Foundations, which had both identified affordable housing as a primary target. These two foundations were instrumental in developing the housing development capacity of the agency over a period of two decades.
- The Fortune Family Foundation, which was instrumental in building the fundraising capacity of Housing Hope. This has allowed us to raise over a million dollars annually for programs which address homelessness.

Q. Housing Hope has attached the word "Village" to many of its housing complexes. Why?

A. "It takes a village to raise a child" has become a well known concept. A village is thought of as a place that accommodates its diverse parts and where villagers watch out for each other. Many residents arrive at the housing complex with few support persons available to them. The spiral into homelessness puts individuals and families in the desperate position of overstaying their welcome with people who offer help. As a result, natural support systems, which we all depend upon at times of need, are lost to these families and must be rebuilt. In some cases the skills to create these support systems were never learned.

A village environment, where residents work together to create a quality place to live, is a beautiful thing. In Housing Hope's model, residents are involved in councils which work to create healthy living environments through shared responsibility where property rules are "owned" by those who live in the apartments. It provides a safe, secure setting for learning and pursuing individual goals. In addition, the housing complex is a vehicle for community support and connections. Our housing village connects with the broader village when children are able to utilize local schools, playgrounds and community programs, and while adults benefit from proximity to faith communities, medical facilities, schools and workplaces. Community volunteers participate at these housing complexes in a variety of ways including hosting holiday events, donating basic supplies and raising funds to assure success of the programs at the site. The end result is residents who feel truly embraced.

Resource Development:
Multiply the fishes and loaves.

Q. What is the concept of leveraging and why is it important to Housing Hope?

A. There are many forms of leverage. Housing Hope is interested in the leveraging of community support for addressing affordable housing and family homelessness.

Leveraging, as Housing Hope has viewed it, is all about finding the fulcrum.

It starts with the notion that individuals and institutions both desire to make an impact with their contributions and investments. They like to see their loaves and fishes multiplied. Contributors take comfort in knowing that there are others supporting an effort. This is partly about mitigating risk but it's also about companionship. Both potential and actual contributors want to be part of something bigger than what they can accomplish alone. Harnessing this desire is the fulcrum upon which the lever multiplies its strength.

This harnessing takes shape in many ways. This involves technical skills utilizing marketing and segmented appeals to the right people in the right way at the right time. Dual leveraging occurs when grassroots contributions are utilized to secure government grants. Governments are much more interested in supporting efforts where significant community participation already exists. And community donors love it when their gifts help secure significant grant funds for their chosen project or program. Usually this process starts with securing local commitments first and then using these to convince a grant maker of the merits of the project.

A good example of Housing Hope's leverage dates to our very first project. First Presbyterian Church provided a $4,500 challenge grant. If Housing Hope could secure a facility for an emergency shelter program it could have this $4,500. This pledge was leveraged to purchase a $233,000 twelve unit apartment building and to secure a $35,000 operating grant for a new emergency shelter program.

Another example is a $1.35 million grant from the Gates Foundation to develop 76 transitional housing apartments for homeless families. Housing Hope's plan involved small neighborhood-friendly housing sites with a mix of homeless families and stable families who needed an affordable long term home. Housing Hope utilized the grant to leverage $36 million of housing and program development at seven scattered locations in the county. This included government grants and a total of $7 million in philanthropic contributions.

Leveraging is about receiving a $10 gift and making it become $100 or $1000.

Q. Why does the community trust Housing Hope with its resources?

A. Housing Hope enjoys great support from individuals, congregations, businesses, corporations, governments and charitable foundations. This derives from two things. First, Housing Hope presents a compelling vision. It is a vision of how to solve family homelessness one family at a time utilizing a locally-based service-enriched housing continuum.

Second, Housing Hope provides effective management. The agency completes what it starts and has a quality product to show at the end of each development process. The project may not finish on schedule and it may or may not finish on its original budget. But every project started by Housing Hope over the 25-year span, for which public or private funds have been received, has been completed. These properties are visible and a credit to the neighborhood in which they reside. Further, Housing Hope obtains independent audits of its accounting, publishes annual reports and provides timely filing of its nonprofit IRS 990 returns to the government. In addition, volunteers witness the organization in action regularly. Timely and transparent answering of volunteer questions generates witnesses to the good practices of the organization.

Housing Hope's good management of public and private resources is well known in the Snohomish County community and beyond.

Q. What's the significance of Stone Soup?

A. Stone Soup, like "it takes a village to raise a child", is a way to discuss community cooperation and collaboration. The children's story tells of hungry soldiers returning from war and how a distrusting village is scared to feed them. But the way worn soldiers offer a vision of a delicious pot of soup that would feed all in the village. The soldier organizes the preparation of the soup in cooperation with the citizens. The soldiers (strangers, in many versions) bring nothing but a pot and their wits. They collect water from nature, and tiny morsels of food from each villager, which combine to make something wonderful which nourishes not only the travelers, but also the contributors.

Housing Hope sees itself as a vehicle for community action on the issues of affordable housing and family homelessness. We are the soldiers who offer vision and management of community resources.

Credits

Building Hope: The First 25 Years of Housing Hope

Published by Housing Hope

Book Steering Committee hard at work

Introduction by Edwin R. Petersen
Manuscript by David M. Buerge
Epilogue by William H. Gates, Sr.

Project Manager: Renata Maybruck
Editor-in-Chief: Edwin R. Petersen
Copy Editor: Brianna Stuart
Editors: Fred Safstrom, Bruce Eklund
Proofreaders: Carol Petersen, Mark Samuelson
Layout and Design: Daniel Thompson, Dykeman
Photograph Coordinator: Diane Smith
Photograph Procurers: Larry O'Donnell, Jack O'Donnell and Kelsey Dosen
Portrait Photography: Kaylee Gervasi
Cartography: Discovery Maps (base map), Kelsey Dosen (graphics)
Writing commissioned by Peter Henning
Printed by Premier Graphics, Bellingham, WA

Paul Vexler, the most "decorated" board member: Board President, Board Member Emeritus, Founding Board Member for HopeWorks

Book Steering Committee:

Pictured left to right back row: Todd Morrow, Mark Samuelson, Fred Safstrom, Bruce Eklund, Jon Witte and Larry O'Donnell. Pictured left to right front row: Renata Maybruck, David Buerge, Diane Smith, Connie Niva and Ed Petersen

Housing Hope and HopeWorks Board of Directors

Name	Elected	Term Ended
Jon Witte, M.D.	1987	1993
Bruce Eklund	1987	1988
Mae Stork Covert •	1987	1996
Amy Youngstrom •*	1987	1996
Todd Morrow •*	1987	1996
Greg Provenzano	1987	1996
Jim Wilkinson	1988	1989
Ron Wilmot •	1988	1997
Todd Wyrich	1988	1991
Wayne Blakely	1989	1997
Nik Halladay •	1989	1995
Carol Jensen •*	1989	1998
Anita Olson	1990	1993
Ben Thomas	1991	1993
Rich Menzel •	1992	2001
Rev Mark Samuelson •*	1993	2002
Greg Starup	1993	1995
Dale Lyski	1993	1998
Frank McCord	1994	1997
Mike Echelbarger	1995	1997
Michelle Frost	1996	1998
Nancy Kniest	1996	1999
Connie Niva •*	1996	2005
Michael Hirai	1996	1998
Judy Lin	1996	1997
Katherine Cook •	1996	2005
Nik Halladay •	1996	2005
Dick Klabunde •	1997	2006
Todd Morrow •*	1997	2006
Fred Safstrom •*	1997	2006
Zoe Hallgren	1997	2004
Margi Layman •	1997	2006
Donna Pedersen	1997	2000
Mary B. Sievers •	1998	2007
Jeff Capeloto •	1998	2007
Jody Ashley	1998	2001
Sharon Hanson	1998	2001
Jimmy Yamauchi *	1999	2001
Joe Ward	1999	2000
Mary Dulin	1999	2000
Bud Brummel	1999	2003
Vida Poling	2000	2002
Janlyn Nesbett	2001	2004
Michelle Sosin Trautman	2001	2008
Bennie Walthall •	2002	2011
Paul Vexler •*Δ	2002	2011
Aaron Lamoureux	2002	2004
Ken Nelson •*	2002	2011
Tony Balk	2003	2006
Dwight Malott	2003	2009
Rick Boies	2003	2005
Judy Rettenmier	2004	2007
Karen Wernli	2005	2010
Maria Schroeder	2005	2007
Bill Yoakum *Δ	2005	
Robert Walker *	2006	
Jill McKinnie	2006	
Bruce Eklund	2006	2007
Jennifer Marvin	2006	2008
Nancy Truitt Pierce	2006	2009
Jim Cosco	2006	2008
Kathleen Horner *	2007	2010
Sarah Duncan *	2007	
Suzanne Britsch	2007	2011
Jimmy Yamauchi *	2007	
Maria Hicks	2007	2010
Dan Clements	2008	2010
Steve Peiffle	2008	2012
Laura Brent Δ	2009	2012
Steve Zwaller	2008	
Andrew Ballard	2008	
Norman Parker	2009	
Todd Morrow •*	2010	
Kathy Burgoyne Δ	2010	
Vikki Strand	2010	
Kathy Moore	2010	
Julie Kestle	2010	
John Dickson	2011	
Leah Schedin Δ	2011	
Tom Fahey	2011	
Nik Halladay •	2011	
Bob Dent Δ	2011	
Patty DeGroodt	2012	

- • *Indicates Board Emeritus (served for 9 years)*
- * *Indicates President's Club member*
- Δ *Indicates HopeWorks board member*

Board President's Club

Pictured left to right back row: Paul Vexler, Kathleen Horner, Mark Samuelson, Fred Safstrom, Ed Petersen, Robert Walker, Bill Yoakum, Todd Morrow, Jimmy Yamauchi and Ken Nelson. Pictured left to right front row: Connie Niva, Sarah Duncan and Carol Jensen

Housing Hope *Award Recipients*

From the beginning, individuals, businesses and organizations that have contributed to the success of Housing Hope's mission have been recognized annually.

In 2001, Stone Soup was converted to a celebration of accomplishments toward addressing affordable housing and family homelessness. It was decided to formally honor three individuals or institutions that had made major contributions to Housing Hope or the community effort toward ending homelessness. One award focused on longstanding support for Housing Hope, while the second recognized housing advocacy and the third honored volunteer commitment.

Pioneer Award - This award is given in recognition of long-term commitment by an individual or institution to the pioneering efforts of Housing Hope. It is awarded in appreciation for sustained, ongoing contributions toward addressing homelessness and affordable housing issues in Snohomish County.

2001 – Mae Stork
2002 – Washington Mutual
2003 – Bob Drewel
2004 – Tim Otani
2005 – Steve Saunders
2006 – Fortune Family Foundation
2007 – Todd Morrow
2008 – Nik Halladay
2009 – Windermere Foundation
2010 – Carol Jensen
2011 – Amy Youngstrom
2012 – The Everett Clinic

Housing Hero Award - Some individuals go "above and beyond" the norm in demonstrating commitment to solving social problems in our community. The Housing Hero award is given in recognition of affordable housing advocacy and dedicated effort at a level that sets an example and inspires the rest of the community.

2001 – Margery Hite
2002 – Shirley Morrow Family
2003 – Windermere Foundation
2004 – Pete Grodt
2005 – Dave Koenig
2006 – Impact Capital
2007 – Mark Lewinski, Kirtley Cole
2008 – Aaron Reardon
2009 – Bud Alkire
2010 – Mary Sievers
2011 – Workforce Development Council
2012 – Seth Dawson

2001 Pioneer Award – Mae Stork (right)

2012 Pioneer Award – The Everett Clinic

2005 Housing Hero Award – Dave Koenig (right)

2009 Housing Hero Award – Bud Alkire

Volunteer of the Year - Housing Hope sees itself as a vehicle for community action. The affordable housing challenges within Snohomish County cannot be solved without the public will of our citizens. It is through the efforts of volunteers that the community is mobilized and Housing Hope's potential as an instrument for creative solutions is achieved. Annually, the significance of volunteer contributions to the Housing Hope mission, is recognized by the Volunteer of the Year Award.

2001 – Ron Wilmot
2002 – Ross Rettenmier
2003 – Ralph Schapler
2004 – Marilyn Komnick
2005 – Mary Carter
2006 – Connie Niva
2007 – John Dickson
2008 – Stanwood Ambassadors
2009 – Carol Baker
2010 – Larry Hanson
2011 – Nancy Truitt Pierce
2012 – Betty Nelson, T.K. Kapelak, Gael Reedy, Janice Tallman, Jo Metzger-Levin and Signature Landscape Services

2002 Volunteer of the Year – Ross Rettenmier (right) with his wife Judy

2011 Volunteer of the Year – Nancy Truitt Pierce

Presidential Lifetime Service Award – The criteria for this commendation from the President of the United States is 4,000 lifetime hours of volunteer service.

2012 - Carol Baker and Joy Cain

2012 Presidential Lifetime Service Award – Joy Cain and Carol Baker

Ten Year Employees –

Ed Petersen *	1987-2012	*Executive Director*
Aat Bontje	1988-2000	*Housing Developer*
Gail Kogut	1994-2009	*Director of Finance & Grants Manager*
Robin Vogler	1994-2005	*Property Manager & Director of Property Mgmt.*
John Sevy	1995-2006	*Director of Housing*
Diane Smith	1995-2011	*Office Manager & Director of Admin.*
Tanya Ward *	1998-2012	*Accountant and Housing Counselor*
Eileen Hinds	1998-2010	*Admin. Assistant and Major Gifts Manager*
Maria Davidyuk	2000-2012	*Childcare Teacher*
David Hansard	2001-2011	*Accountant and Director of Accounting*
Robert Del Rosario *	2001-2012	*Accountant*
Carol Williams *	2001-2012	*Accountant and Director of Accounting*
Karen Matson *	2002-2012	*Case Manager and Director of Services*
Linda Swanson *	2002-2012	*Case Manager*

* *Current staff member in 2012*

Index

A

Adams, Doug - 98
Ambler, Sue - 105
American Jewish Service Society – 44, 51
Arlington, City of – 47-48, 65, 69, 71, 73, 76, 85, 87-88, 103
Arlington Action Committee – 47, 87
Arlington Triplex – 48, 54
Avanti House – 70, 114
Avondale – 92-93

B

Balk, Tony – 84-85, 135
Bank of America - 100
Beachwood – 67, 73-74, 93, 102-103
BECU – 108
Bill and Melinda Gates Foundation – 83, 87-90, 103, 118-119, 143
Blakely, Wayne – 29, 135
Blue Spruce – 47, 69
Boeing – 23, 39, 43, 45, 49, 61, 107-108
Boeing Employees Good Neighbors Fund (BEGNF) – 40, 43, 62
Bogart Meadows – 76
Bontje, Aat – 32-33, 36, 55, 57-59, 62, 75, 91, 137
Boyle, Martin - 84
Braun, Jim - 75
Buerge, David - 117, 134
Build, Serve, Sustain campaign – 83, 91, 93
Building Credits – 60, 65

C

Calvary Lutheran - 50
Cascade Bank (Everett) – 44, 49, 57, 65, 90, 96 98
Creating Access to Careers in Healthcare (CATCH) – 107, 143
Central Lutheran Everett – 14, 16, 21-22, 25, 27, 39-40, 44
Century House – 54-55, 65, 70-71, 75, 88, 142
Coast Real Estate Services – 91, 106, 108-109, 111, 143
Cocoon House – 51, 70, 86
Cole, Charles – 38-39
College of Hope – 83, 90, 94, 102-105, 118, 127, 143
Commerce Bank – 30
Commerce Building – 59-61, 64, 78, 93, 142
Commerce Cleaners – 78
Community Health Center – 51, 102
Compass Health – 20
Cook, Katherine – 56, 135
Cooper, Dr. Tom – 90
Copper Station – 97, 111
Country Manor – 73
Craven, Bob – 71
Craven, Kathy – 71
Crossroads – 29-31, 33-35, 37-38, 40-41, 43-44, 56, 61, 66-68, 77, 108, 127, 142

D

Deaconess Children's Service – 55, 102
Dean, John – 37-38
Delores and Floyd Jones Courtyard - 113
Dent, Bob – 43, 107, 108, 135
Dickson, Bob – 75, 83
Dickson, John – 83, 135, 137
Domestic Violence Services – 51
Dotson, Michael - 100
Drewel, Bob – 49, 74, 81, 137
Duncan, Sarah – 114, 135

E

East County Branch – 85, 87-88
Eklund, Bruce – 7, 15, 21-22, 27, 95-96, 111-112, 115, 134-135, 142
Everett, City of – 10-18, 20-21, 24, 26, 28, 30-38, 40-41, 44-46, 49-50, 55, 57, 59, 66, 69-73, 75-78, 81-82, 84, 87-88, 92, 98-99, 102, 106, 110, 115, 130, 142
Everett Community College (ECC) – 105-106
Everett Gospel Mission – 20, 24, 51, 55, 62, 93
Everett Mutual Bank – 44
EverTrust – 83

F

Father William Treacy – 37-38
First Congregational Church Everett – 32
First Methodist Everett – 22
First Presbyterian Everett – 12, 15, 22, 28, 30, 54-55, 71, 75, 132, 142
First United Methodist – 13, 22, 29, 50, 72
Fortune Family Foundation – 81-83, 96, 108, 131, 136, 143
Fortune, Cay – 81-82
Frederickson, Kay – 67
Frontier Bank – 34, 44, 75, 83, 98-99

G

Gates Sound Family Initiatives – 100
Gates Sr., Bill – 88, 118-119, 134
Gold Bar – 46-47, 53, 59, 142
Granite Falls, City of – 47, 54, 69, 76, 88
GroundWorks Landscaping – 36, 108-109, 143

H

Haywood, Veronica – 84, 86
Helseth, Grady – 71-72
Henning Family Learning Center – 112-113
Henning Jr., Peter – 112, 115, 134
Henning, Janice – 75
Henning, Mark – 108
HoopJam – 90
Hope Builders – 35-36, 43, 83, 127
HopeWorks Social Enterprises – 36, 78, 83, 101, 105, 107-110, 114, 127, 135, 143
HopeWorks Station – 109
Horner, Kathleen – 99-100, 110, 135
Housing Hope Properties – 46, 50-52, 56, 85, 127
Housing Hope Village (HHV) – 9, 58, 74, 77, 92-93, 107, 109, 112, 142-143
Housing Opportunity Fund – 52, 93, 142

I

Immaculate Conception Catholic Church Arlington – 22, 29
Impact Capital – 59, 62-63, 85, 91, 126, 136
Index, City of – 84-85
Interfaith Association of Snohomish County – 51, 62, 93

J

Jensen, Carol – 38-39, 43, 50, 77, 87-88, 135, 136
Jonasen, Mary – 107, 109
JP Morgan Chase – 98, 108

K

Kantor, Mark – 60
Keep Hope Alive campaign – 66, 76, 80, 83, 90, 127-128, 142
Ken Schilaty Family Learning Center – 94, 103, 143
Kennedy Court – 41, 43-44, 54, 56-58
Kennedy, Bruce – 41
Kennedy, Dorothy – 41
Kestle, Julie – 114, 135
Kids Clinic – 51
Kirtley Cole – 86, 98, 136
Klabunde, Dick – 80, 135
Kvagnes, Deirdre – 67

L

Lake Alyson – 47, 54, 59
Lake Stevens, City of – 22, 70-73, 76
Lake Stevens Action Committee – 71, 85
Lamoureux, Barb – 66-67, 82
Larson, Bob – 47
Layman, Margi – 71, 77, 135
Leach, Jan – 38-39
Leone, Bret – 90
Lervick Family Village – 68, 88, 142
Lervick, Arne – 68
Lervick, Ida – 68
Lewinski, Mark – 86, 136
Lincoln Hill Village (LHV) – 93, 112-114
Locke, Gov. Gary - 74
Lombard Apartments – 36, 41, 49, 57
Luther Child Center – 11, 28, 32, 35

M

Maple Leaf Meadows – 87
Marvin Gardens – 111
Marysville, City of – 67, 72-73, 88, 102, 114
Marysville Action Committee – 72, 72-73, 85
Matson, Karen – 109, 137
McCord, Frank – 44, 49, 65, 75, 135
Medina Foundation – 40, 78, 83, 94
Mental Health Services – 20, 25, 28, 34, 44, 77
Menzel, Rich – 50, 135
Mignacco Mansion – 57
Mission Highlands – 110
Mobley, Nancy – 70
Monroe, City of – 41, 84-86, 92-93, 98, 103, 111-112, 114, 143
Morrow, Shirley – 15, 22, 24-26, 50, 136
Morrow, Todd – 7, 15, 26-29, 41, 56, 64-65, 77, 89, 102, 114, 116, 134-136, 142
Mt. Baker View – 106-107, 114

N

National Equity Fund (NEF) – 59-60, 63-64
Nelson, Ken – 96, 99, 135
New Century Village -71, 92-93
Niva, Connie – 28, 30, 75, 80, 82-84, 89-90, 92, 102, 116, 134-135, 137
North Branch Board – 38, 87-88
North Snohomish County Association of Churches (NSCAC) – 6, 21-22, 24-27, 30, 35, 48, 89, 93
Northwest Children's Fund- 40, 42, 142

O

Oakes Avenue Commons – 76, 78-80, 93
Olson, Anita – 22, 35, 135
Opus Bank (CA) – 98
Otani, Tim – 53, 98, 136
Our Saviors Lutheran – 16, 22, 35, 68

P

Park Place Townhomes – 114
Peace Lutheran Silvana – 47
Petersen, Carol – 14, 16, 18-20, 22, 32, 51
Petersen, Ed – 14-16, 18-25, 27-36, 38, 41-42, 45-48, 51, 56-59, 62, 64, 66-67, 71-75, 77-79, 81-84, 86-87, 91, 93-96, 98, 100-102, 109, 115-116, 134-135, 137, 142
Piasecki, Dottie – 75
Private Industry Council (PIC) – 42, 48, 102, 105
Pigeon Creek – 8-9, 74, 115
Pioneer Bank – 29, 44, 52, 98, 142
Port Susan – 87, 92
Prins, Lori – 51
PropertyWorks – 105-107, 143
Provenzano, Greg – 29, 65, 135

R

Rettenmier, Judy – 76, 135, 137
Rettenmier, Ross – 76, 90, 137
Richards, Jack – 73
R.K. Dent Transitional Housing – 107
Rodriquez, Pastor Vic – 73
Rowe, Pastor Rudolph – 72

S

Safstrom, Fred – 44, 57, 80, 90-91, 95-96, 134-135
Samuelson, Rev. Mark – 21, 22, 25, 77, 89-90, 134-136
Saunders, Jo – 68
Saunders, Steve – 13, 136
Schilaty, Flo – 94
Schilaty, John – 94
Schilaty, Ken – 94,
Scott Foundation – 40
SeaFirst Bank (Stanwood) – 39, 93
Self Help Housing – 33-34, 45, 53-54, 59, 64, 69, 76, 78, 87, 91, 97, 103, 105, 110, 116, 142
Seventh-day Adventist Church – 42
Sevy, John – 61-62, 64, 79, 91, 95, 112, 137
Shimer, John – 81-82
Sievers, Mary – 83, 135-136
Signature Landscape Services – 108, 137
Simon, Candy – 28, 34
Sky Meadows East – 93
Sky Medows West – 93
Smith, Diane – 114, 134, 137
Smokey Point, City of – 69, 71, 87, 103, 114
Southwick, Mel – 77, 112
St. Cecelia's Church Stanwood – 37-38, 47, 142
Stanwood, City of – 37-39, 41, 47, 50, 54, 65, 68, 71, 76, 85-88, 92, 97, 103, 112-113, 115, 142
Stanwood Ambassadors see Stanwood Action Committee – 38, 68, 87-88, 137
Stanwood Action Committee see Stanwood Ambassadors – 38-39, 47, 50, 68, 73, 77, 88
Stanwood House – 41, 50, 142
Stave, Barb – 22, 35
Stone Soup – 39, 53, 82-83, 87, 90, 94, 99, 114, 133, 136, 143
Stork, Mae – 7, 13, 21-22, 25, 27-28, 30, 34-35, 46, 59, 112, 135-136, 142
Sultan, City of – 85-86, 92, 98

T

Ten Degrees – 105-106, 114, 143
The Bluff at Arlington – 87, 93, 103
Timber Park – 69
Tomorrow's Hope Childcare Center (THCC) – 42-45, 51, 55, 57, 61-62, 65, 74-75, 77, 83-84, 93-95, 102-103, 114, 127, 142
Trinity Episcopal – 22
Tulalip Tribes – 110

U

U.S. Bank – 52
Unger, Tom – 43
Union Bank – 98-99
United Way – 28, 34, 43, 49, 71, 77, 102, 125

V

Vexler, Paul – 101, 110, 113-114, 135
Volunteers In Service to America (VISTA) – 25, 28, 30, 34, 44-45, 78, 90, 103
Volunteers of America – 20, 51, 62, 84-85, 93

W

Washington Mutual Bank (WAMU) – 52-53, 98-99, 103, 131, 136
WaterWorks Irrigation – 109
Wells Fargo Bank – 52, 93
Whitehorse Foundation – 83
Wilmot, Ron – 29, 31, 34, 36, 135, 137
Windermere Foundation – 66-67, 83, 98-99, 131, 136
Windermere – 29, 36, 66-67, 98, 127
Winter's Creek North – 86, 93, 98
Winter's Creek South – 86
Witte, Jon – 7, 16, 22, 25, 27, 41, 84, 134-135, 142
Woods Creek Village – 93, 98, 112
Workforce Development Council – 105, 136

Y

Yamauchi, Jimmy – 90, 114, 135
Yates, Roy – 75
Year 13 educational model – 103-106
Youngstrom, Amy – 7, 12, 22, 27-28, 31, 35, 56, 135-136, 142
YouthBuild – 105, 143
YWCA – 51, 62, 85-86, 93, 102

Housing Hope *2012 staff*

Staff displays apparel from 25 years of Housing Hope history

Twenty-Five *Significant Events 1987-2012*

1 — June 1987

Association of Churches — The North County Association of Churches convenes a Housing Task Force, which recommends the creation of a new nonprofit Housing Development Corporation.

2 — September 30, 1987

Founders — At a lunch hour meeting Housing Hope is founded by Amy Youngstrom, Todd Morrow, Jon Witte, Mae Stork, Bruce Eklund and Ed Petersen.

3 — 1988

Emergency Shelter — A 12 unit apartment building in the Rucker Hill area of Everett is purchased to offer emergency shelter for homeless families.

4 — 1989

Housing Opportunity Fund — A new housing predevelopment fund is created with help from Pioneer Bank, through Nik Halladay and Ralph Schapler.

5 — 1989

Stanwood — St. Cecelia Catholic Church of Stanwood contributes $454 toward the Housing Hope mission, which the Board of Directors uses to initiate a Stanwood shelter and housing program. With support from the Stanwood Ministerium a single family house in Stanwood is purchased.

6 — 1989

Childcare Program — Northwest Children's Fund provides $10,000 toward the start of a childcare program for Housing Hope residents. This starts the journey toward creating the Tomorrow's Hope Childcare Center.

7 — March 1993

Teen Parent Program — First Presbyterian Church of Everett pledges $50,000 toward the creation of a new facility to serve homeless women who are pregnant. A house on Everett Avenue (Century House) is dedicated, which begins the homeless teen parent program.

8 — 1993

Self Help Housing — USDA funds Housing Hope's sweat equity home ownership program. The first group of eight families complete construction of homes on a city block in Gold Bar.

9 — 1995

Commerce Building — Housing Hope's first tax credit project is completed in Everett with the renovation of a downtown historic office building resulting in 48 new housing units for homeless, low-income and vulnerable individuals.

10 — 1994-1998

Building Hope — Housing Hope builds capacity and raises funds in a $1.5 million capital campaign (Lervick Family Village and Housing Hope Village.

11 — 1995

Tenth Anniversary — Housing Hope celebrates its first ten years with a grand opening of the Housing Hope Village facility as its new headquarters.

12 — 1999-2000

Keep Hope Alive — Sustainability of the housing program is addressed through a community fund drive to create a $1 million Endowment Fund to take care of Housing Hope's properties.

#3 – Crossroads

#8 – Rambler from Self Help Housing

#11 – Ribbon cutting at Housing Hope Village

#15 – Society of Hope Membership Key